The "ON" Position

The "ON" Position

The Sexual (Mis)Adventures of a Hollywood Journalist

KATIE MORAN

VOLT PRESS

Chicago and Los Angeles

09   08   07   06   05   5   4   3   2   1

Library of Congress Cataloging-in-Publication Data

Moran, Katie.
    The "on" position : the sexual (mis)adventures of a Hollywood journalist / Katie Moran.
        p. cm.
    ISBN 1-56625-225-3 (alk. paper)
    1. Sex—United States. 2. Sex customs—United States. 3. Women—Sexual behavior. 4. Single women—Sexual behavior. I. Title.

    HQ18.U5M67 2004
    306.7—dc22

                                                          2004010335

Volt Press
A division of Bonus Books
875 North Michigan Avenue
Suite 1416
Chicago, Illinois 60611

Printed in the United States of America.

*To Robert and Michael . . .
and to all of the individuals
who have lost the fight against AIDS*

CONTENTS

The Electrician

Because the title of this book is *The "On" Position*, it seems fitting that the first chapter should be dedicated to that ever-popular device . . . the vibrator. Owning one is nothing to be ashamed of—I have four of them. What woman doesn't have one? Owning up to it is another story.

Since the time of Hippocrates women have been diagnosed with "hysteria," a disorder associated with lack of orgasm. In other words, these women were not getting off enough, so they sought medical attention. It was a common practice to go to a doctor for a "pelvic massage," which was basically a legal hand-job, until the 1880s, when vibrators became all the rage. Upon learning this little tidbit, I finally understood why my great-grandmother called them "the good old days."

Doctors hated the lengthy and exhausting procedure of

getting a woman off, thus leading to the invention of a mechanical device to speed up the process. Stimulation by way of a vibrator was only available through a doctor and many physicians began making house calls with portable, battery-operated devices in the early 1900s. Can you imagine this phenomenon? "Go outside and play for a while, kids, Mumsy is busy with the doctor . . . don't mind the buzzing . . . it's nothing. Oh, and if you see Daddy coming home from work, be sure to run ahead and knock on my door!"

By 1918, vibrators were available to the general public and advertisements for them were seen in the back of the Sears catalog, a vague description camouflaging their true use. It was not until the 1970s that vibrators were openly advertised as sexual pleasure devices.

My friend Sheryl is a stunning brunette with flawless features, a master's degree, and a great sense of humor; a woman who should be able to have sex with any man any time she pleases. However, recently Sheryl hit this almost comical dry spell and she just could not get laid. She had no problem getting dates; it was just that she could not get any one of them to actually stick it in her. Finally Sheryl went on a date with a guy who she considered a real "turn-on." He was exactly her type: tall, rich, and Jewish. After a great evening, Sheryl brought him back to her place, where he noticed that the light in her bedroom wasn't working—so he offered to fix it. The only plug she was interested in testing was the one in his pants, so she rolled her eyes while he played handyman with the lamp. It had been eight months since Sheryl had gotten laid and she was now antsy, but she waited patiently for him to finish the sincere gesture. Eventually her date thought he had found the problem, so he yanked on the cord to wiggle it free, but instead of her lamp, he pulled the wrong cord and sent a pink object flying—Sheryl's vibrating dildo, which she kept stowed under the bed.

The gasps from both Sheryl and her date were so loud that

they nearly covered the sound of the giant pink snake squirming and buzzing across the hardwood floor. A few moments later, the handyman politely excused himself from Sheryl's life. Another failed date—but at least "pinky" was here to stay. Sheryl would need the company after a night like that. She felt a panic attack creeping up on her as tears welled in her eyes. She felt helpless and wondered, "Why can't I get a guy to sleep with me? What's wrong with me?"

Like Sheryl, many women rely on vibrators and other "toys" to masturbate. Recently my brother's friend Brenna drove to Los Angeles to visit for the weekend. Her husband, a sailor, had been sitting on a ship in the Persian Gulf for eight months. They were newlyweds when he left the country and Brenna, a hyper-sexual girl to begin with, was absolutely dying with desire. She had barely said her hellos to us before she was on the phone calling sex shops in search of the latest model of her favorite vibrator, a rotating pearl-handled instrument that moved at least ten different ways. The vibrator she sought had far too many options for me, but Brenna swore by it. After several calls she scribbled down an address, grabbed her keys, and piled us into her little yellow beetle. She sped down darkened, liquor store–infested streets on our mini road trip to a very seedy sex shop. Within the blacked-out windows was an array of dirty-haired male customers looking at the impressive collection of porn through blood shot eyes and shifting nervously in their cheap tennis shoes.

Half the fun of going to trashy sex shops is the fear of getting shot on the way inside. This particular place was as bad as they get; there was a drug deal going down on the corner and outside the door crackheads were begging for change. I don't know about the rest of my party but I was turned on! We asked the proprietor of the shop, a tiny Asian woman in her mid-thirties, where to find Brenna's special vibrator. She smiled and said, "Right here, oh very good, very, *very* good!" I asked her if

Katie Moran

she had tried it and my brother punched me in the arm. The woman just giggled as I turned away, imagining her hanging out in the back room of the sex shop going to town with the pearly rabbit vibrating wildly against her clit.

Picturing people in sexual situations is a habit of mine, probably because I am a very visual person. It is a fun quality to have but can cause problems; when someone is describing something revolting like stepping barefoot in poo I immediately picture it happening to me; I smell it, feel it and then my stomach turns and I gag. I love to hear about sex but the best blowjob story in the world is ruined if it's my mother telling it! When something like this happens I usually retreat into a lost space within myself. Either that, or gag.

Back in the sex shop I finally snapped back to reality but the little Asian woman had walked away. Brenna found the item she was looking for, a $100 dildo with pearls spinning about the shaft—the Mercedes Benz of vibrators. She also bought me a string of purple anal-beads. I kept taking them out of the brown paper bag they were in and imagined using them. (I have used the beads since then and I think buying and fantasizing about them was more fulfilling than actually using them. During sex, I was worried that when we were done with them my partner would pull them out and there would be poo on them and then, of course, I would gag. My guy friends call this a "shitsicle" . . . the surprise they get when they pull their penis out of a woman's ass and find more than they bargained for.)

We got back to my brother's house and Brenna immediately went upstairs, saying "I am going upstairs to masturbate, please don't come up for at least fifteen minutes." I admired her boldness. Fifteen minutes later, she came down, freshly showered with a peaceful smile across her face. A few minutes later my brother's friend Camron, a tall good-looking guy of twenty-five, went upstairs saying, "Don't come upstairs for at least an hour . . . I am going in the hot tub." And that was that. The night turned into an open, yet private, masturbation session. I like to call this blatant masturbation. Blatant masturbation is when someone masturbates openly, usually in front of or obvious to those they are close to. One of my cousin's friends would sit in front of a three-way mirror and admire his penis, stroking it and viewing it from all angles. If someone would walk in the room he would softly say, "It's beautiful, isn't it? Would you like to touch it?" Um, no thanks.

The experience of that night was definitely new to me. My brother and I were raised in an environment where everything was private; private parts, private rooms, private lives, and doing things "in private." That night changed things; it gave me the go-ahead to share something that even the mention of is usually kept intimate. Of course, I knew my friends masturbated but I never really knew when, and I certainly wasn't in the next room reading a magazine waiting my turn. As the night went on, another friend followed Camron into the hot tub. My brother and I stayed downstairs to catch up on gossip; he had just flown back from Italy and we hadn't seen each other in months. Neither of us joined in the masturbation going on upstairs; the idea of blatant sexual activity anywhere near a relative is really a turn off. I guess my family privacy held up in some respects.

My close friends and I have always talked openly about masturbation; we all have our own style and personal preference. One friend of mine keeps her gigantic "back massager" out in the open so that visitors basically trip over it on the way to her bathroom. Others shy away from toys altogether. I have friends who are really skilled with their own hands and can manage an orgasm in under a minute, kind of like a guy. That's not me; manual stimulation takes way too long and I find it frustrating. Plus, I have bad wrists from typing on my laptop all day. I can only imagine how bad they would be if I were using them for masturbation as well!

Katie Moran

Every woman that I know wishes she could be a guy, just for day, to feel what it is like to have a penis. The number one reason for this desire is not the ease of urination, sex with a woman, or any other societal or emotional reason. No. Women want to know what it feels like to jerk off. How great would it be to wake up and be able to stroke something large (hopefully) on the outside of your body? I think I would be tempted to play with it way too often. I would want to whip it out in public or rub it up against people, kind of like the guy on a Paris subway who backed up against me and took his little, over-played-with stub and got in a few wanks before being pulled back to his seat by another passenger. I would end up getting arrested for indecent exposure. I don't have a penis, and incidentally, I don't even have a large clitoris so if I was a guy I would probably have a real average-sized penis. I'm glad I am a woman because that is one less thing to worry about.

My best friend in college was Kristina, a woman who loved phone sex. Kristina was a very sexual girl, always horny. She masturbated at least six times a day and even carried a pocket rocket vibrator to work with her so she could masturbate under the desk. She bought batteries by the case for that thing. After our nights of drinking she would go home and call me late at night wanting me to entertain her with dirty stories. I went along with it straining to keep my eyes open and fighting exhaustion as the morning crept up on us as she wanted to go one more round. I would have preferred some actual physical contact; still, these conversations stirred my active imagination and brought up brilliant visuals of her lying on her bed forcing a vibrating device into her crotch, gyrating her hips, and fighting her need to scream out in ecstasy. This was not sexy for me, but it was entertaining. It was only the beginning of my education about other people's sex lives.

The main problem with these vibrating phone sex sessions was that Kristina lived at home with her two very religious, older parents in a small, thin-walled beach house. This did not stop her from masturbating; I think it might have made her more fanatical about the whole thing. Kristina was twenty years old and a heavy drinker yet still very much under her parents' control. She had two DUIs in one year and would regularly come home in the early morning intoxicated and wreaking of cigarettes. Understandably her parents were not happy about Kristina's behavior and they decided to try to reel her in. It put a major damper on our social lives.

As a punishment for her being caught with marijuana, Kristina's father took her bedroom door off its hinges; she now had no privacy. For a girl that masturbated six times a day, this was a big problem. A few weeks later Kristina called me; she was drunk from downing two buckets of Malibu rum and Diet Coke at her favorite Hermosa Beach bar. She got on the phone with me and whispered in a breathy and sensual voice. I muted *Saturday Night Live* on the television and asked, "Did you light candles? Where are you?"

"I am in bed. I am taking off all my clothes, putting on my Enigma CD and . . ." I heard a buzzing sound. Her vibrator was on. I started telling her about a couple I had seen having sex on the beach in Santa Monica; and soon I had her going pretty good. All of a sudden I heard the phone drop and the muffled sound of her down comforter ruffling. Then I heard a man's voice. Her father! With no bedroom door to stop him he had walked right into the room to ask her a question and found her laying there, candles lit, music playing, vibrator buzzing . . . and on the phone with me. Poor Kristina. If that did not kill her libido I do not know what would. She did not get her bedroom door re-installed for several months after that. It was definitely time for Kristina to get her own place.

It is impossible to be an avid masturbator when there are people invading one's privacy constantly. Unless of course you are a confident guy like my friend Mamu. Mamu takes his dick

Katie Moran

out at random and jerks off at parties, sleepovers, and beach trips; he has no shame. One college roommate of mine in the dorms would say that she was brushing her teeth with an electric toothbrush while she was actually using her vibrator in the bathroom instead. She was in there for up to twenty minutes sometimes. I guess that explains why she had bad breath.

I only masturbate when the mood is right. I can go a long time without even thinking about it, especially if I am in a relationship and having regular sex. As I mentioned earlier, I am not much of a manual girl; I like the toys. Fortunately, the market is flooded with really cool devices that can rotate, swivel, or vibrate. There is even a new toy that actually penetrates by moving up and down. I have yet to try that one, but I have spent time at countless sex shops, absorbing all the new colors and sizes available. The general consensus from all the women I know is that a simple vibrating head or bullet and a couple of fingers slid into the vagina in the right place does the trick. Whatever your preference, it doesn't really matter as long as it gets you there.

Buying a vibrator for the first time may be embarrassing for some. My favorite place to shop is a dimly lit sex shop where they check ID; I prefer this to the large supermarket-style Hustler store on Sunset Strip in Los Angeles. I am glad, however, that the Hustler store is there because it puts sex and sex toys out in the open, making them acceptable and fun. Of course, if you want a little more privacy, there are plenty of online stores to choose from. I bought my large, purple, vibrating monkey, Charlie the Chimp, from www.clubparadox.com. It came discreetly delivered in a plain box and the service was very good, in more ways than one.

Recently I was assigned a story about sex toys. Part of my assignment included going to a dildo factory in San Francisco. All I had heard about Vixen Creations was that they made only high-quality, silicone products and that the company was owned by a woman who had worked for years at Good Vibrations, the popular sex toy manufacturer. I didn't know what to expect as I drove through a slightly deteriorated neighborhood on a typically foggy May day. As I pulled into Vixen I was greeted by a pack of friendly dogs; inside, the factory was just as welcoming. Vixen was clearly a family environment; the employees all wore shorts or jeans and T-shirts and as they worked they peered up over the heads of giant purple and white marbled cocks to smile at me. The owner of Vixen was a hippy-ish woman in her fifties; the other women walked the thin line between butch lesbian and what my friend Bobby calls an MQM, short for "Man Question Mark," as in, "Hmm, is that a *man . . . ?"*

I was in absolute awe as I stepped further into this artist's domain. It was beautiful. Shelves lined the walls, each one filled balls to head with multi-colored dildos. They were everywhere, some already wrapped in plastic, others still dripping wet from being washed before being packed and shipped to the next lucky recipient. The first group of toys I happened upon was a bunch of very squishy, flesh-colored flaccid penises. I asked what THOSE were for . . . they were so small and limp. My host didn't give me an answer but I could tell by the look on the face of one of the more butch lesbians that they were used for "packing." Packing is the term used when women go out with a fake dick in their pants. Some women I know even go so far as dressing like men and wearing tighty whities to hold their fake packages in place. These fakes were brilliant; I could almost feel the peach fuzz that grows under a set of testicles. I closed my eyes and gave it a good feel, wondering if I would be fooled if I came across an MQM in a bar and reached for this package. Nah, not me, I thought. One of the women looked at me with a tough-guy Pacino expression. She asked, "Do you like it?"

I blushed. "Yeah, it feels real. I could get into it."

Katie Moran

Al looked at me, pushing for more. "Do you like dick?" she asked.

"I don't discriminate," I said, rubbing the shaft of an even larger faux penis. "Do you like it?" I asked her.

She put a firm palm over the silicone dick, squeezed it, and replied, "I like *this* one!" With that we both laughed.

The factory was much larger than I had expected, and as I continued on with my tour I was amazed at all they had to offer. Their most popular item is a double-ended dildo called the Nexus. They have two models, one large and one junior. The larger-sized model is marbled in black and white and is not the typical double-header; it can be used with or without a harness and is anatomically correct with one end designed to stay put while the other is angled for penetration. Moving along I admired a table full of anal plugs; some were huge and painful looking, others were made in sparkly colors and looked like something a Barbie doll would have as a toy.

The next room of the factory housed the molds. All of the dildos and toys were hand poured into the molds and also pulled out by hand. I yanked a giant purple dildo out of a mold, stretching it until I thought it would snap. It came out with a pop and quickly bounced back to its original shape of a swinging penis pendulum. Along the back wall of the warehouse was a row of washing machines that clean all the products.

The most interesting room was the "wet" room. The paint and silicone were mixed in the wet room and there seemed to be just as much color on the floor and walls as in the large white buckets. It felt like stepping into a rainbow. I love the smell of sex toys, probably because it reminds me of sex and pleasure, so I really enjoyed being in this room. So much so that I turned around and realized that everyone had moved on to the next room and I was still standing there looking wide eyed at all the colors as if I was on some sort of strange drug trip.

The "On" Position

After the tour of the factory, the ladies gave me a demonstration of all the various attachments that could be used with a bullet vibrator. They plugged in a very powerful vibrator and demonstrated the options including a fascinating bright red tongue and a big-eared fox. The most popular attachment was the Gee Whiz, a dildo-like attachment that fits over the head of a giant Hitachi vibrator. One of the women looked at me directly and softly said, "Touch it" as if it was attached to her. I did and it felt incredibly powerful. I am quite sure I would have gone numb in a matter of seconds if I had that much vibration going on down there.

Before I left, I was given a brown paper bag of sex toys as party favors. My gifts included a Nexus Junior, the smaller blue-and-white version of the larger one I described earlier. There was also a silver-metal-flake-sparkly butt plug in the shape of a three-inch cock, a large-sized chocolate brown dildo, a dark purple anal plug that was a factory defect, and a blue-and-white marbled dildo shaped like a string of pearls. I could not wait to go home and try the Nexus out myself; I had other plans for the remaining gifts.

My aunt, Julia, is always my host while I am in San Francisco. She is in her forties, gay, very "out," and has led a wild life full of partying, drugs, traveling, and women. During my summer vacations from college I would often go visit her. My friends and I would go into the city, go to three different clubs or bars, hit a strip club, and finally come home only to find her and twenty friends in a giant cloud of various types of smoke, laughing and screaming in her living room. Sometimes I'd join them for a game of cards or to share a story and then go to bed only to find them still there the next day, still drinking and feeding the constant cloud of smoke. Julia and I have a great time together, even doing things as simple as driving through the city sightseeing and making up fake identities for the people we see in the crosswalks and on corners. We drive through

Katie Moran

Chinatown, stop for lunch, buy idiotic hats in the Haight that we force each other to wear, and flirt with waitresses. In short, we act completely immature together. Before I left San Francisco I gave Julia one of the dildos as a thank you for driving me to my meetings in the city. She called her girlfriend Rain on the walkie-talkie mobile phones they both had. I heard a loud BEEP . . . then, "Yo baby! I got a BIG BROWN DILDO just for you!"

Julia was having trouble with Rain at that time. Rain is a big woman, slightly older, but with the same smoker's voice as Julia and a history of drinking a bottle of whiskey before verbally abusing everyone in sight. For this, she was on my shit list. It is so inappropriate to yell at someone or belittle him or her in front of another person, especially a member of their family. Rain had no shame. Julia told me that Rain liked to be fucked with big brown dildos and that her dream was to own an Accommodator, a dildo attached to a chinstrap to be used during oral sex. Rain had been talking about owning one of these for the five years I had known her, yet she had never purchased one. I do not understand this mentality. If I want something, I buy it, especially if it is something as cheap as a chin dildo. Come on. But this probably sums up Julia's tortured existence as the girlfriend of the unsatisfied Rain, the woman who would not buy her dream dildo.

The night before I was to go back to Los Angeles, Rain and Julia had a massive fight and Julia hid the new brown dildo so that Rain couldn't find it. She was going for dildo depravation, I suppose. By the end of the night, a full throttle dyke fight had erupted, complete with bottles being thrown or smashed against walls and doors punched in while hip hop music blared in the background. The big brown dildo became a weapon of destruction by evening's end and I fought to keep from breaking out into hysterics as Julia pummeled it against Rain's fat jowl, knocking the drunken woman to the ground, as her eyes rolled back in her head.

The final item in the paper bag created another drama all its own. It was a purple butt plug called the Tristan. It has a unique shape that supposedly stays in the ass better than the average anal toy that can slip out (and always does) during sex . . . or with a mere sneeze, cough, or laugh. I gave this toy to my gay friend Bobby, the typical looking-for-love-in-all-the-wrong-places, overly idealistic, and charmingly romantic homosexual male. He had just gotten over his last relationship with the love of his life, Adam. The recovery period from this relationship was long; he was still avoiding parties that Adam was at nearly two years after they broke up. But, of course, they were in love and it had been serious; they had had six wonderful days together.

Bobby had finally found a new guy, Blaine, and the whole thing seemed too good to be true. They had met at the Starbucks on the corner across from the LA Fitness on Santa Monica Boulevard, a coffee joint so packed with fags that it makes one wonder if any gay men are gainfully employed and where; since they all seem to spend their days sipping chai lattes and chain smoking Marlboro Ultra Lights on the Starbucks patio.

On a Friday night in West Hollywood, Bobby took Blaine out on his dream date. First, they went to Starbucks (of course) and then drove four blocks to the movies to see *Legally Blonde 2* and then flirtingly shared Chinese food off of each other's plates. Later, they went back to Bobby's to conclude the evening. What happened next almost ended our friendship, even though I bought him a Starbucks gift certificate for ten lattes to apologize.

Bobby hadn't gotten laid in two years since he and Adam split, and Blaine was his big chance to finally get some back-door action (Bobby was a bottom). I encouraged Bobby to try out his new butt plug but he was apprehensive about introducing sex toys in the bedroom on a first date. However, after a mood-altering blowjob, Bobby displayed his new special toy to Blaine who excitedly shoved it up his own ass. Well, as I

Katie Moran

---

mentioned before, the anal plug was slightly defective. Blaine's happy groans turned to screams as the butt plug gravitated up his anal cavity, locking in place somewhere in his rectum. The base of the plug had completely vanished from view!

Blaine jumped out of bed and locked himself in the bathroom; all Bobby could hear were a few "owwws" and "uuuhs." Finally Blaine came out of the bathroom pissed off like an old queen who had lost her wig. His bow-legged limp told Bobby that the piece of rubber had not been dislodged. Blaine yanked on his Diesel jeans and wife-beater tank, slipped into his Puma sandals, and was out the door, Jaguar keys in hand. Bobby ran after Blaine, chasing him down the hall wearing nothing but a sheet. He bumped into the manager of the building, an older Greek man with back hair who had been trying to bed Bobby for years. Bobby escaped and caught up with Blaine, coercing him back into the apartment. He carefully undressed the furious Blaine and used a lubed finger to attempt to wedge the anal plug out. It would not budge. When they were just about to give up, Blaine sniffled and complained to Bobby that he had given him the flu. He let out a giant cough and the anal plug shot to the ground, only to be scooped up by Bobby's Chihuahua Rusty, who carried it into the kitchen chewing on it all the way there.

Vibrators and sex toys can aid women and men in achieving orgasm, with or without a partner; the first step to really enjoying the experience is letting go of any shame attached to using them. I have a friend whose mother is horrified at the mere mention of a vibrator. She says they are "disgusting" and "wrong." But let's face it, when used alone, a vibrator is safe sex!! If I had a teenage child, I would prefer to find out they were masturbating with toys rather than having unsafe sex with multiple strangers. If you happen to be a person who has not purchased or used a toy due to shame or embarrassment, here are a few tips that helped me get comfortable with them.

The "On" Position
─────────────────────

First, find a sex store that is far enough from your home to guarantee you won't run into any of your mother's friends. I went to one in another state. I browsed the store for hours and read the backs of the packages looking for any information that would help my selection. (When I bought my first toy, a double-ended dildo, the Internet wasn't so widely used as it is now.) I suggest looking online, as the selections are incredible at most sex toy outlets and manufacturer's Web sites.

Next, talk to friends who you know or suspect might use them and start a dialogue on the subject. If you are in a relationship and want to introduce toys into the bedroom, feel out your partner and ask what their comfort level is—then share all your own desires. A good way to get rid of a guy you do not want to date any longer is to show them your dildo collection. I went out on a date with a lawyer named Mike who was so boring I actually feared a second date. He wanted to come in after the date to "see my house." I gave him a tour and some coffee for the long road away from me that he would be driving home that night. When he was in the bathroom, I ran into my bedroom and pulled out this gigantic double-ended dildo. It wasn't even something I used; it was part of my friend Mia's Dirk Diggler-from-*Boogie Nights* Halloween costume. I then positioned the dildo so the tip peaked out from under my four-poster bed.

When I showed Mike to the bedroom I coyly said, "Oh my, how did this get left out?" I pulled the massive dildo out from under the bed and let it dangle from my hand in all its thirty-six-inch glory. Mike turned white; he couldn't hide the expression on his face. I had never encountered this level of disgust from a man like that before. He downed his coffee and left with one of those weak fake hugs. I never heard from Mike again. When men can't measure up, they usually walk rather than step up to the plate. I couldn't blame the guy; I got my wish, he didn't call, but who could really compete with thirty-six inches anyway! He must have felt like my friends and I feel when we

Katie Moran

see the gigantic anal plug, which has a base bigger than a bowling ball, at the sex shop. It sits on the pedestal in the center of the store and the clerk says people actually buy and USE it.

So why did Sheryl's date flip and take off so quickly? Embarrassment is the most likely answer, but quite possibly he was intimidated like my boring date, Mike. Sheryl's vibrating dildo was quite a bit larger than the average penis. Sheryl is able to laugh about the situation now that she is settled in with her new boyfriend. They even use the vibrator in their own sex life. And the other guy? Some men just can't handle a little competition.

2

Firsts to Remember

There are a lot of firsts in a woman's life: first kiss, first love, first time having sex, first time having sex from behind . . . everything seems so amazing when it is new. What would it be like if every time was just like the first? Well, the first time having sex is usually only exciting because most women are thinking, "Oh, my God, I can't believe I am finally having sex!" At least that was what I was thinking when I lost my virginity. Otherwise, it was just awkward and a bit uncomfortable. No one really briefed me beforehand on the fine art of moving the hips, thrusting, and squeezing the Kegel muscles. Even if sex had been explained to me first, I would still think practice is the only way to fully understand it.

I received a phone call a few days ago from Heather, a young friend of mine who is still in high school. She wanted to lose her virginity worse than anyone I have ever met; she had been trying to find a guy to have sex with for the past year. She wanted my advice on how to get a certain guy to sleep with her. Now most girls I know don't adopt this attitude until their late teens or early twenties. In fact the majority of the high school girls I have encountered try not to have sex for the first time until they meet the "right" guy, usually a serious boyfriend who might pressure them or talk them into sex. It is rare for a girl to persistently and actively seek this out at the age of fourteen or fifteen; at least it's rare in the upper-middle-class suburbs of Los Angeles and Orange Counties.

My youngest brother is still in high school, and, although he is one of the most popular football players and is fawned over by all the girls, he can confirm that a teenage girl does not seek out getting laid. For most teenage girls who have sex in high school, it just kind of "happens." Girls are far more secretive about their sex lives in high school than in later life, mainly because the sexually active ones are not inclined to share their experience with friends who are still virgins or they are fearful of earning a reputation as a slut. Teenage boys actually talk about pursuing sex or even joke about finding someone for an unfortunate pal who hasn't met anyone to have sex with. I won't pretend that I understand the culture of schools where thirteen- or fourteen-year-old girls get pregnant; many such schools have condom programs and even nurseries for the students' babies. I do know enough, however, to realize that teenage sex can be and is a serious problem in many schools and communities, especially when accompanied by a lack of education or an environment where children do not know any other alternative.

I had no desire to be sexually active in high school; sex was absolutely frowned upon in the Catholic school that I attended. Beyond the social implications, I just wasn't physically ready at age fifteen like Heather was—I had no sex drive at that age. Her quest mirrored that of a teenage boy's desire to get laid for the first time; she was horny and obsessed. I had told her months earlier that it was no big deal and it was really better to wait, but she was dead set on finding someone to do it with. All I could advise her to do was find someone nice that she was friendly with; someone that she could feel comfortable with and order around a bit and not feel pressured by, and to use a condom. She wanted to have sex with a twenty-five-year-old that taught surf lessons at the local beach. Luckily, he knew better than to de-virginize jailbait. She finally found a guy named Greg who was willing to sleep with her one Saturday night when she threw a party at her parents' place. They had sex in her bedroom while her parents were in their room, watching TV. The girl had some balls to have underage sex when her parents weren't even out of town. I would have been too scared to even go into my room alone with a guy for fear they would knock at any moment.

There are different styles of parenting, but also a lot has changed in the last ten years. Parents are so afraid of what can happen in the outside world that they are letting their kids drink at home and have people of the opposite sex over rather than let them go out. One of my aunts let her teenage son grow weed in his closet because she knew he was smoking it and did not want him to waste money on it or get caught buying it. I asked Heather how her first time was and she replied, "It was small, it hurt, and it only lasted for three minutes." I told her that my first time was quite similar except that it was big, it hurt, and it lasted for three minutes.

"Does it get better?" she asked.

I had to think about that for a second. "It can, but you might meet that same dick in another body somewhere down the line."

"FUCK!" she replied.

One of the greatest firsts of all, however, is when your

Katie Moran

partner gives you the first earth-shattering orgasm of your life. This kind of orgasm will make your whole body explode—you may lose consciousness briefly, take a ride to the top of the stars, and melt away into pure ecstasy. The best way to accomplish this is by finding a skilled and giving partner. Make sure you are extremely attracted to him or her, and make sure to hit that G-spot repeatedly in just the right way. There are countless great books on how to achieve orgasm so I will not dwell on that subject. I believe it is different for every person but at the root of this success and pleasure is self-confidence and the ability to let go. People who are insecure and self-conscious rarely achieve orgasm.

Austin was the first man I ever had a real orgasm with. It was amazing; we had taken a walk down the street near my house and stopped by the side of the road to kiss. We were both so turned on that we almost had sex right under the streetlight; I was wearing a skirt so it wouldn't have been too difficult. He grabbed my hand and we ran to my home. By the time we burst through the front door we were both breathless. We fell on the nearest object, an armchair, and had the most frantic and spectacular sex I had ever had in my life.

I remember meeting Austin at a bar while I was out with Kristina. She had gone to high school with Austin's brother so he recognized her and sat down with us. I barely even noticed him, I was too busy checking out the buddy he brought with him, his next-door neighbor, Sean. Sean was more my type; he was kind of slick-looking with dark brooding eyes and a troublesome smile. I thought he was right up my alley. At that time, just out of college, I was the quintessential party girl. I made the rounds, knew everyone at the door, and was given free drinks at every bar I frequented. Sean seemed up to speed but Austin was too quiet and reserved and he dressed like he honestly didn't care. It turned out that he was not one of those guys who dressed and looked like he didn't care because it was hip; Austin truly did not care about the way he looked or what other people thought about him. He drove an old Tercel that didn't have a radio, just a space with wires where the radio had once been. I will explain why this point is important later in the book.

A couple of days after meeting Austin and Sean, I called Kristina to ask for Sean's number. She didn't have it but gave me Austin's number instead so I called him and asked for Sean's number. I was amazed when he refused to give it to me. Not used to getting turned down, I demanded to know why. He said, "Because I want to go out with you. How about we go out and if you don't like me, I'll give you Sean's number." I liked his attitude and anyone who could stir my curiosity deserved a date.

A lot of my memories about my relationship with Austin are vague due to the excessive drinking and partying I did at that time. I was twenty-one when we got together and I still behaved like a college senior. I kept a bottle of middle-of-the-road vodka in the freezer, a twelve-pack of Coronas in the fridge, two bottles of wine in the cabinet, a pack of Parliaments on the coffee table, and a few buds of marijuana in a dresser drawer. I would pretty much do any other type of drug that someone offered me if the mood struck me, I just didn't keep anything else in stock.

Our relationship suffered greatly due to my habitual party going, bar hopping, and all-night carousing. At the time I didn't think I was doing anything wrong, but in retrospect, I can see how hard it must have been to have a girlfriend like me. I was the kind of girl who stumbled through his door drunk at 4 AM, tasting of drugs and liquor, demanding sex yet covered in the perfume or cologne of someone I had made out with for the night. In my defense, some of this behavior grew out of the desperation that Austin would not commit to anything serious with me. He lived in his parents' house, never referred to me as his girlfriend, and constantly talked about moving overseas to pursue writing or hockey. He ended up leaving the country for three months to live in Spain and play hockey in a European league. Our relationship was the best it had ever been while he was gone because he was forced to communicate through letters. He sent me the most amazing letters. It was the first time I had ever seen his handwriting; it was small and precise, very masculine and sexy.

For my birthday he sent me a letter with a gram of blonde Spanish hash tightly rolled up in it. I had never smoked hash (another first) and I was excited to try it, so I packed it into a marijuana pipe and lit it like you would light some bud. Soon smoke was billowing out of my room and into the adjoining hallway; I was staying at my parents' house for the weekend but they were in Florida so I wasn't worried about it. Unlike pot, which burns up fast, this hash kept going and going . . . and going. Before I knew it, I was trashed and the bowl was still lit.

At this point I could barely see, but it seemed like the hash was out. I dumped the ashes into the trashcan in the bathroom and lay down on my bed. I stared at the ceiling and dreamily noticed that the cloud of smoke was at least a foot thick on the ceiling. I wasn't sure if the cloud layer was expanding by the minute or if I was just really high and tripping, but when the smoke no longer smelled of hash and turned into chemical fumes, I knew there was a problem. I ran into the bathroom and stared at the trashcan. It had turned into a fiery inferno, burning from the top down like a massive cigarette. The fire was fast burning and angry as it made its way to the carpet. I stumbled to the sink and filled a glass with water and dumped glass upon glass of water on the fire until it had subsided. The house stunk for weeks and when my parents returned from vacation they were welcomed with brand new bathroom flooring installed by yours truly. Austin inspired many firsts, but two I'd prefer not to repeat were my first time almost burning down a house and the first time laying bathroom tiles.

Although I loved his letters and his gifts from Spain, I missed Austin and his flawless body. Even off the ice I could visualize his muscles stroking a puck into a net. His company wasn't too bad either. When he finally returned from Spain, it was back to the way we had left it except the nights were filled with even more incredible sex and even fewer words. As relationships go on longer and there is no natural progression to the next step, whether it is moving in together or saying "I love you," it is fairly obvious that the end is near. At the time I did not want to believe it was going to end, probably because the sex was so good. But there is something inside all of us that has this intuition. We can choose to tap into it or ignore it. In this case, I felt we were growing apart but I never addressed it.

My friend Georgia claims she can hear an imaginary "click" in her head when a relationship is ending. According to her this sign can be so clear that the click is audible from across a room. A military man she had been dating for a year invited her to a very important family party at the home of his uncle, a senator. She was thrilled and thought this might be the occasion when Brian, her boyfriend, would propose to her. The party was held in a beautiful garden setting and Brian joyously introduced her to all of his immediate and extended family. Georgia had a giddy smile on her face all evening, she felt sure she was "in." At sunset Brian's uncle proposed a toast. He raised his glass high and, with the same broad and welcoming smile that Georgia was wearing, he looked over his guests, thanking them for attending his gathering. He then turned his attention to Georgia and, putting his arm around his nephew, bellowed for all the guests to hear, "And let me introduce everyone to the most wonderful woman Brian has ever brought home, the lovely Georgia! Here's to hoping we will be having a wedding for them soon right here in this backyard!"

Katie Moran

Then everything froze in time. Brian stiffened and the smile fell from his face. Georgia was deaf to the cheers of the crowd as she zoomed in on Brian, feeling as though she was tapping directly into his brain. "CLICK." There it was. She knew everything was over. Within four days their relationship had folded.

For me, the signs were not as clear that things with Austin might be heading for splitsville. Austin's mother liked me and wanted to see us together. His parents would take us out on their boat, his mother mixing us strong cocktails and making us laugh. Austin and I would sneak on that same boat late at night in King Harbor, Redondo Beach, and have sex in one of the beds onboard. No matter where we were, the sex was amazing. One funny thing about us is we never had oral sex; Austin didn't like it and we both quietly agreed that it wasn't necessary. It was never missed. Having sex with him was an out-of-body experience, time and time again. The times when I hadn't had a drink or smoked a joint were still just as mindless and explosive. He was a hockey player with an agile style of fucking. His thin torso could move independently of the rest of him, moving in directions and angles that seemed only possible by contortionists. There was not an ounce of fat on him. He would become rock hard in seconds and stay that way until I was duly satisfied. I could have as many as six or seven orgasms and often thought that he was having an orgasm inside me when in actuality I was having one. He would ask, "Is it all right if I come now?" I would reply, breathless, "Yes, thanks, that was great." The relationship with Austin produced another first for me, and I'm sure that all women can relate to this one—the first time getting dumped.

It sounds ridiculously dramatic to say that Austin was the only man I had ever been in love with, especially since I was only twenty-two at the time. But it must be true because it saddens me a tiny bit even today that we broke up. It was the definitive turning point in my love life, and I think that all people, both men and women, have that moment; that stabbing pain when your soul tells you, "This can never happen again!" It only took getting hurt really badly once for me to shut the door to that overly trusting, naïve part of myself. First loves are truly amazing. Every time you are with him or her you feel like you have never been happier and you want the moment to last forever. It's completely delusional, but it happens.

I have a guy friend named Seth who experienced such severe emotional pain early on in life that it took him eleven years to trust a woman again. Because one woman screwed him over, dragging him from state to state before smashing his heart, dozens of women have suffered the wrath of his charms. Although Seth is a really honest guy and tells women right up front, "I don't want a girlfriend, just sex," most women still get sucked in and think that they are somehow different.

I suppose it is no surprise that Austin, the man who sparked these intense emotions in me, was also the one who turned me off. But first, he turned me on . . . on like never before. I don't know if it was his generous size or the fact that he never said more than two words at a time that made him so sexy. Certainly his ability to stay hard for more than two hours and help me on my way to six orgasms in one night did, indeed, have something to do with my being "in love" with him. Okay, so it might have been a sex thing. I couldn't help falling in love with someone who could fuck so well. But have you ever had it so good, so cosmically, mind-blowingly good that you kind of just ignore the little things? Little clues such as big road signs telling you that the relationship is ending?

As I walked up the long drive to Austin's beach house, I noticed that his car was packed with what looked like all of his belongings. Did he get in a fight with his parents and decide to move out? I slowly took a few steps closer to the entrance of the house and saw a U-Haul trailer hitched to the back of his car. Being that he is a rather cheap kind of guy (remember, no radio in his car) and that renting one of these things had to set him back a hundred or so, the situation must be serious. When I walked into his house, it was empty except for his bed, which he was sitting on. He was moving. We had dated for nearly two years and he was moving to Colorado.

Excuse me? He never told me a damn thing about it! I had no idea he was moving until I saw the packed car that night. Was he going to let me know as he backed out of the driveway with a turned head, a honk, and a wave? This was so unbelievable. Austin was never any good at confrontation, but this was just insane. Why couldn't he talk to me about it? I was experiencing an utter lack of communication. I had never needed him to talk much but this was beyond unacceptable.

In a way I am grateful for the way things ended. I have broken up with many people in my time and I find it so hard to leave, probably because I forgive too easily. I found three ways to make breaking up a lot easier to swallow. Number one is hate. Hating a person is a great way to get over a relationship. If it is real hatred, you cannot stand that person and the sight of them makes you sick. It is perfect and you think to yourself, "Get me away from this guy!" My very good friend Emma called me a couple of months ago when her baby was two weeks old. She sounded somber and distant, as if her voice was miles away. She said she needed to ask me for some relationship advice and brought up a court case in which a cheating husband was convicted of killing his pregnant wife. She asked if it was typical.

I said, "What? No, killing your pregnant wife is not typical!"

And Emma replied, "No, cheating on your wife while she is pregnant with your baby."

My heart sunk; I knew what she was referring to. I've had far too many women introduce me to their new boyfriends, men who have recently left their pregnant wives or wives with newborns.

Many men cheat on their pregnant wives and I had always suspected Emma's husband, Jay, of being an avid cheater. Once while working on a story we were both assigned to, I walked into a hotel room that the crew was sharing to find a nineteen-year-old girl sitting on his lap. I had no proof, but the fact that Jay works in the sex industry as a cameraman for some of the wildest crews in the world raised my suspicion. I sat in silence on the phone with Emma as she sadly recounted the story about the day she went into labor with their son, a child that he had wanted more than she had. She called his cell phone and it took him five hours to show up at the hospital for the birth of their first child. While she suffered complications and had to have a cesarean section, he paced the halls outside the delivery room, on his phone with his new girlfriend, a washed-up old Playmate who looked like a strip of beef jerky on Q-Tip legs. Horrid. Emma gave birth and he left the hospital the moment the child was born. He never returned to the hospital, not even to pick her and the baby up. He finally came back to the house five days later.

Emma was in both physical and mental pain by the time Jay came back with the obvious hotel receipt in his pants pocket. I guess he wanted to get caught, and finally he did the only thing he knew how to do, and it wasn't creative or even admirable in a scumbag-underhanded-motherfucker type of way. We would have at least been entertained if he was caught, like another friend of mine, because her new lover sent flowers to her boyfriend's house instead of hers! And even Emma admitted it would have made more sense if the woman he cheated on her with was attractive, perhaps one of the current supple Play-mates. Instead, he chose one of the ugliest Playmates to ever sprawl across the glossy pages. Perhaps unsurprisingly his new girlfriend is a married woman and her husband was on to her from the beginning.

We found out a few weeks later that the Playmate's husband

Katie Moran

had a private investigator follow her all the way from the East Coast, taking photographs of the affair and documenting her credit card spending. I suppose for her being caught on a cross-country cheat-a-thon has a certain amount of style to it, but Jay is just a loser. He was cheating right in front of his wife's face; he had even tricked Emma into going out to lunch with "Butterface," a nickname Howard Stern gives to a girl who has a great body, "But Her Face" is hideous. With his total lack of concern for his wife and terrible timing, Jay can be described as nothing short of a cocksucker.

I am fine with the fact Jay wasn't in love with Emma anymore and wanted to leave her but he should have followed a couple of the rules of good break-ups. Firstly, don't get your soon-to-be-ditched wife pregnant; and secondly, if she does get knocked up, wait until the child is at least six months old and the wife is recovered from the birth and able to find a job and take care of herself. As it was, Jay left Emma with nothing except a mortgage, a newborn, and a surgical scar; a broken heart, a dog, and a laundry list of insults and put-downs. One night Emma's son was so sick that she couldn't leave the house to pick up medicine, so she called Jay to ask him to go to the pharmacy. He hemmed and hawed but finally agreed to pick the medicine up on his way to dinner with another one of LA's biggest losers, the owner of one of those straight-to-video, girls-flashing-their-tits type shows. Emma's phone rang, and it was Jay. He had left the medicine on the doorstep and took off.

At that moment Emma realized that she didn't want to be with Jay. No amount of love they once shared could make up for what he was doing to their son. Jay was too selfish to be a father to the baby and basically abandoned him; he was creating history, as Emma puts it. He never came to visit and he never asked how the baby was doing. Emma replaced any love she had for Jay with hate. She realized she could never forgive him. The hatred Emma had for the person Jay had become made it that much easier to realize that this break was for good. She promptly served him with divorce papers and closed escrow on their house.

The second easy way to speed toward a break-up is cheating. Of course, cheating can spur on hatred, as in the case of Emma and Jay. I always hate someone if they have cheated on me and I don't even look back when we break up. Of course, if the roles were reversed and I had become the cheat-ee instead of the cheat-er, then my partner would probably hate me too. I would certainly hate myself; and I would know it was over because the trust would be gone.

I knew a woman who was pregnant by a man who was cheating on his pregnant wife. She said she was approaching her mid-thirties and wanted a child; I can only assume that she was lonely and desperate. I thought it was pathetic to embrace a man that did not belong to her. She was hurting herself, his wife, and his new baby by being with him. The only married man you should ever sleep with is your husband, only the desperate sleep with other people's spouses.

I have had my own share of cheating men; I was dating a motocross rider who went by his last name, Schott. I don't even remember his first name. He pursued me for months and finally wore me down to the point that I gave in and went out with him. Schott had a child and an ex-girlfriend, a bitter and controlling little woman who glared at me from the corner of her eyes; I could swear she was putting a curse on me! Schott and I went out on several dates but I never felt that close to him, something was holding me back. I was over at his house one night while his two-year-old daughter was there. The little girl hated me and looked at me with the same dirty look as her mother. Usually kids absolutely love me so her obvious dislike was pretty disappointing. The child dropped my car keys in my lap as if to say "GO" . . . and I did. I left that night and never saw Schott on a dating level again. We remained friends

Katie Moran

because we worked together but I turned down his offers for future dates.

Later I found out that he had lied to me; the whole time we were going out he was still with his girlfriend. He was cheating on her with me! I was so horrified that I was deceived and I felt so bad for this poor woman. About a year later I ran into him and his best friend and Schott asked me out on another date. His best friend confirmed that Schott's girlfriend had finally accepted that he was a cheater and they had really broken up this time. I still turned the date down, not because I didn't like Schott but because he cheated. Even though he did not cheat on me, just knowing that he cheated on another woman was enough for me. My personal policy is to always boycott cheating men.

The third way to make a break-up easier is to move. My friend Mia has had two major break-ups in her life and they both involved cross-country moves. She takes these drastic measures because she knows she cannot return. With long-distance separation, there are no one-nighters, break-up-to-make-ups, accidental run-ins, or final things-to-settle that bring you back together and so on and so forth. Mia left her fiancé Vincent a month before their wedding and took off from Texas to California. She left her house, her friends, and her fairytale planned-out life. She even left the dog.

Once Mia arrived in Los Angeles, she never looked back, and it took years before the two could even talk or consider becoming friends again. I asked her why she had basically fled the state to end the relationship and she explained that it was the only way to make a clean break of it. She said that if she was far enough away Vincent couldn't come and try to change her mind. She immediately filled her life with other men, emotionally unavailable types looking for a good time and finding it with her, a bird just let out of its cage to take flight. And Mia flew high, sometimes too high. She partied to a self-destructive degree. It really was as if a wild animal was on the loose.

Vincent was heartbroken and stayed single for years, still in love with Mia. But Vincent eventually moved on, met a girl, fell in love, and now has a three-year-old daughter that he adores. He wouldn't have had her if he and Mia were still together. Mia went on to date a male model that was so insanely gorgeous he made all the women and at least half the guys stare wherever he went. He was literally straight out of a magazine, featured in Calvin Klein and Ralph Lauren underwear ads, just to name a few. Mia had a similar party girl existence that I had in my relationship with Austin. In this case, however, Mia's partying had become so severe that Darius, her boyfriend, left to go live overseas (in Spain, incidentally) because he "didn't want to see her destroy herself." Mia was heartbroken but not as tortured as if he had just left her to go live down the street and date the blonde next door.

In life everything happens for a reason and you never know when something better is waiting for you around the corner. Who would think that when your self-destructive party-going drives away your supermodel-boyfriend that you will pick yourself up from your bootstraps and move on with your life? That you'll clean up your act, get a job, and several years later bump into a hot TV star who promptly goes gaga over you? Mia finally met the love of her life, the kind of man she never thought she would end up with but whom we all knew she deserved. Mia is best friends with my friend Bobby and he and I get giddy when we think about the gorgeous couple up in their giant home in the hills, dog and cat snuggled by the bed, watching movies and admiring each other's beauty. Love is a truly amazing thing. Maybe that is why it is so life-changing when it ends.

But what happens when there is no hate, no cheating, and no leaving? How can a relationship end when you still like the

Katie Moran

person but just don't want to BE with them anymore? I asked my mom this very question and she told me to refer to Paul Simon's song "50 Ways to Leave Your Lover." Since "Go out the back, Jack" is pretty much the same as moving or running away, I still felt confused. I guess that is why people often get stuck in relationships even though they do not think it is best in the long run. That, and the fact that a lot of people do not move out of relationships until they have a new person lined up, even if they have been thinking about leaving for a long time. I often twiddle my thumbs and fantasize about one day moving on, but have a hard time taking the big step and actually doing it. I also have a hard time hurting another person's feelings; I say I am leaving but one tear shed by my partner and I am right back to where I started.

Some women become extremely depressed after being dumped. I know women who lose weight (I wish that were me, like most women I can pack on a few pounds when I am dumped), drive around aimlessly in their cars listening to sad music, or go on massive party binges, drinking away their sorrows. When Austin broke up with me I was determined not to give him that much; I never cried over him, I just made damn sure to never let another man hurt me again. I became the insensitive prick in relationships with men for a good while after that—even if that was only what I dared to show on the outside.

Break-ups have the ability to change us. They shape how we will act in the next relationship. And getting dumped can make a woman a little more protective of her own heart. Sure, she may move on and she may even grow from the experience in a positive way, but what implications does this have on her feelings? The first reaction is to personalize the break-up. The typical self-doubting questions pop into a woman's mind: "What's wrong with me?" and "Why am I not good enough?" or "Is it because I don't swallow?" Do not listen to those harsh judgments we all put on ourselves. Sometimes things just don't work out. And really, no matter how many quick "fixes," such as food, new lovers, exercise, hobbies, and stalking come into play, the only real cure for a break-up is time. Shopping, pedicures, full-body massages by guys named Lance . . . and time.

Katie Moran

3

Sliding Out of the Closet

have always considered myself to be a girl with a pioneering spirit. As James Dean said, "I don't consider myself a homosexual but I am not going to go through life with one hand tied behind my back." Bravado is just the beginning of having fun and adding adventure to your life. This was the case for me. The same feeling that drove me to try alcohol for the first time, to get on the back of a rodeo horse, and to get in a car with one of New York's biggest drug lords (not all in the same day), is the same itch that led me to where I was about to go next.

By the time I reached my senior year in college, I realized that there was one thing I wanted to try but had not. The feelings that spurred on my adventures thus far are also the same feelings that kept me from doing something dangerous and getting hurt. The rush of adrenaline, the shortness of breath, the fear . . . a split-second decision can change the course of a person's life. But if we never try the things that intimidate us, we will never learn. I would never have tried to jet-ski when I was seven and developed a passion for it. I would never have sent my first story to an editor and had it published. I would have never adopted a stray dog with a slightly annoying habit of viciously biting my face but who ended up becoming a best friend. None of these things would have happened had I succumbed to my own nervousness. How different would life be if we did not walk a fraying tightrope once in a while? I wanted to try it all. So, the next intimidating thing on my list to try was . . . pussy.

I have always been a little bit fascinated with the idea of being with another girl. It started when I was in second grade and another little girl, Mandy Helmes, would kiss me during spelling class. She would put two folders up on either side of our faces and we would kiss each other on the lips. That was probably the first time I was ever sexually aroused. Mandy Helmes was the most popular girl in school and I liked the attention the most; the fact that she chose me made me feel empowered. It may have been her blue eyes or her Bonnie Bell lip gloss that contributed to my fascination, but in retrospect I am sure it was the scandalous aspect of the whole exchange. The experience had such an impact on me that when I hear the name Mandy, I ask what the last name is in the hopes that it is her. I often wonder what her life turned out to be like . . . did she get married and have children? Did she become a hot bartender in a cool club? I knew it was wrong; children were not supposed to have any contact in class, especially at my tartan-plaid-wearing suburban Catholic school. And I was taught that boys and girls kiss; girls do not kiss other girls. We were repressed.

When I first saw two kids kissing behind the lockers, my first reaction was not, "Oh neat, a voyeuristic occasion to see some girl on boy action!" It was more in line with "I cannot believe what they are doing. How disgusting. I should go tell the teacher so this does not happen again. What if a first grader sees this and starts crying?" I never went as far as ratting the kids out, but the shock factor of sexual behavior among my peers was something that stuck with me for many years to come. I was seventeen and in my first year of college before I snapped out of the Catholic "sex is bad" mindset.

I loved doing things that were wrong and I have spent my entire life proving to myself that if something feels right, how can it really be bad? I knew it was more of a thrill to kiss Mandy than listen to my tired eighty-year-old teacher's false knee click when she walked to the chalkboard. I know several women who say that their obsession with the same sex started at a very young age. My friend Patty, a sassy, bleach-blond, un-employed actress from Dallas, used to chase around a fellow kindergarten girl who wore a Winnie-the-Pooh belt and smelled like vanilla ice cream. Another one of my girlfriends took things a step further while playing doctor with her best friend; the two of them performed oral sex with each other at age eight. She said she even had an orgasm. The sex between them became habitual, just like little girls playing Barbies or boys riding bikes.

No matter how many times I hear my friend tell this last story, I am still amazed. I take this piece of her life and arrange it every which way in my mind to see if it will ever make sense but it never does; I am utterly shocked each and every time. I hear stories like this all the time from women who were sexu-ally exploring before the age of ten. What? Did these women not have enough Lincoln Logs and Legos to keep them busy?

I, on the other hand, lived in the land of the sexually chal-lenged and did not even know where my clitoris was until I was on my eighth or ninth sex partner. My interest in women con-tinued through junior high, where I would stare at my social

Katie Moran

studies teacher's breasts as she leaned over my desk. I was a solid B student, so my mother never questioned my desire to have Miss McConnoughy come over to our house to tutor me. Good old mom chalked it up to me being overzealous about my studies. My childhood remained void of any and all sexual exploits until the age of thirteen when I had my first French kiss with a hot water-polo player who also let me wear his letterman jacket and took me to horror films, just to hold my hand. The only fantasies I had about women were deeply suppressed and only apparent in the pornographic cartoons I drew and passed to my friends during high-school Shakespeare class.

Though I wasn't doing anything, my friends and I were open to talking about sex from a young age. We devoted hours to writing dirty stories about the nuns having lurid affairs with the school's janitor, Paco. I attended an all-girls Catholic high school—need I say more? Reports of lesbian activity were a constant joke on the campus for the simple fact that there were no men around. If two friends were too close, then rumors would spread that they were gay. It was not a big deal for me even then, as my exposure to a lot of gay men and women granted me an enormous amount of acceptance for both individuality and sexual preference. I knew firsthand that gay people were okay, safe, nice, and not to be feared. I was blessed to reach adulthood having a broad view of so many different people's sexual preferences.

A lot of people never realize that being a homosexual is not "bad" or "wrong." The most common thing I hear in an argument about this subject is "but it's just not normal!" And I have to think, "Well neither is marrying a drunk and slapping your kid across the face but you seem to do that every other day!" Really, how behind the times are these people? What is *normal*? My friend Mariah and I speculate that being "normal" is just a combination of suppression and denial. How boring to be normal. I have yet to meet one person that I would consider normal. This is what makes up our diverse existence; this is what makes each one of us unique. If there were a set norm, life would be monotonous and depressing.

Although I am accepting of other people's sexuality, I will be honest and admit that I like gossiping about their exploits. Come on, who doesn't like to spread the word! I have always liked to hear a good story about someone getting blasted at a baseball game and screwing someone on a first date in the stadium bathroom, or someone else sleeping with a married man. During high school I had a particularly slutty friend named Liz who would get drunk at every party and have me drive her car home. The next day she would call me asking, "How did I get home?" This happened nearly every Friday night. Sometimes she would lean her entire body out of the car window, ass on the windowsill, hands holding on to the roof rack, topless, big breasts bouncing in the wind. This would have been fine except that we were on one of the busiest streets in Hollywood and her audience was a car full of cops. Luckily, we did not get stopped.

At one of our graduation parties I noticed a line of about twenty high school guys leading into the bushes. They all seemed horny, yet very nervous. I peeked around to find Liz giving one of them a blowjob. Incredibly, she remained in the bushes for hours and ever since that night she was fondly referred to as "Line-up Liz." While I may not be the girl who gives twenty blowjobs in one night I am the girl who loves hearing all about it. I never thought any less of Liz for her choices, although I found it sad that she did not remember most of them. At the age of seventeen, Liz was the first person I knew to make out with another girl. She did it in front of everyone at, of course, a graduation party. The rumors spread rapidly about her escapades and not a week went by that summer without hearing a new Liz tale.

I admire people that can live a life free of gossip and have

Katie Moran

some sense of privacy, but I tend to thrive on verbal openness in an almost exhibitionistic fashion. My one rule is that I will never break someone's confidence. When I say gossip, I mean sharing experiences that I have had or listening to friends tell me their adventures. Sometimes I will be having some out-of-the-ordinary sex and all that is running through my head is a list of people that I want to tell about it the next day. I had sex with one guy that I had been wanting to fuck for a long time; and I remember walking him to his car carrying my cordless phone in my hand with my thumb on the number eight (the first number of my best friend's phone number) ready to call her the minute he pulled out of my driveway. It was like it had not happened until I had repeated it to my best friend, so obviously I thoroughly enjoy telling stories about sexual exploits and affairs.

I had acceptance for others' so-called deviances yet I had very little self-acceptance in my late teens. It was okay for other girls to sexually experiment with the same sex, but the thought of actually having sex with another woman repulsed me. I was a late bloomer, more of an observer than an active participant in sex and relationships; the thought of giving a guy a blowjob turned my stomach until I was almost twenty-one. And, for the record, sometimes I feel like I am the only twenty-eight-year-old woman who has never liked a man enough to let him come in my mouth. My best friend is so dedicated to her boyfriend that she said she would swallow any bodily excretion he had and enjoy every moment of it. She even watches two consecutive football games on Sundays for him! I am not that willing. Is that the lesbian in me manifesting in my straight re-lationships? Quite possibly. But the whole act of swallowing just screams "Biohazard!" No thanks.

I come from a family in which three uncles and an aunt are homosexual. My earliest childhood memory is of my Aunt Julia picking me up from school and letting me drive her classic '60s

Mustang, the headliner ripped out, crayon drawings of the Rolling Stones tongue logo covering the roof and dash, and a pit bull lying in the back seat. Julia lived in Venice Beach with her girlfriend, Shelly. She was a tough kid. My mom said that although Julia was eight years younger than she, Julia was having sex with women way before my mother had even lost her virginity.

Both my godmother and godfather were completely out to me at a very young age. I used to wonder why Uncle Matty wore silk shirts and would always show up at Thanksgiving dinner with a cologne-soaked Puerto Rican guy—not that it bothered me. He was the most fun of all my relatives, dancing all night to loud disco music and roaring with laughter at any joke.

Los Angeles (thank God) is a very diverse and accepting place to grow up. My friend Patty, the girl from Dallas, grew up with the notion that it was not okay to be gay. In fact, it was so looked down upon by her parents, family, and friends that she has spent her twenties stuck in miserable relationships with men because she was taught it was wrong, or taboo, to be with a woman. And because she was adopted, she lived in complete terror of not being accepted, of being tossed aside by her family if she did not live up to their expectations of perfection. Her first relationship with another woman was the most beautiful thing to witness; I looked forward to hearing every detail of their courtship. To watch her fall in love for the first time was like watching a butterfly shed its cocoon and emerge in its new body to explore the world. When they finally broke up, it was devastating to watch. Surprisingly, the problem in their relationship was not Patty's past issues; it was due to the fears her girlfriend harbored, placed on her by her stern and judgmental father.

Patty was thirty years old before she finally allowed herself to be with a woman. Many women find out what it is like at a

Katie Moran

much younger age. College is a playground for all kinds of experimentation, though it took me till I was a senior to find out for myself what it was like to be with a woman. Sure, the nine mixed drinks probably spurred on the evening, but it was something that was bound to happen and had been in the making for a long time.

My best friend in college, the avid masturbator Kristina, was a girl with enormous breasts and the highest rate of liquor consumption of any human being I had ever met. She was definitely a "fun" girl, we had been friends for three years and it never grew boring. I loved being around Kristina and was completely infatuated with her before the sexual attraction set in. As a child I had this strange habit of idolizing older girls; I would write poems for babysitters and draw pictures and cards for them. Looking back on it, I can see a pattern in my frequent obsessions with slightly older girls. Kristina was only a few months older but she was bolder, bigger, and much more popular than I was. I nicknamed her Senator Sullivan because she knew everyone on campus. We were unable to walk from one building to the next without a ten-minute conversation with one of the many guys smitten with her.

I kept to myself in college. My roommates were already in grad school so I mostly hung out and went to bars with them. Kristina was different than my other friends. She made me feel like all of her friends were mine as well; she made everyone feel that way. She was the kind of girl that looked at you with giant eyes and a tilt of the head, her huge smile radiating warmth for miles. I get butterflies and a lump in my throat just thinking about her today. She'd put her arm around everyone she came in contact with and made them feel comfortable and relaxed. Her blonde and voluptuous beauty made her look like a version of the young Brooke Shields with a dash of sultriness like the skinny Anna Nicole Smith. Kristina made me feel a spectrum of emotions I had previously reserved only for men. When she looked at me her eyes penetrated the surface going straight to my soul, leaving me breathless, just as my first love Austin had. The feelings were so similar that after a while I didn't even realize that she was a woman. Her gender no longer mattered; it was the sensation of powerlessness over my intense feelings that I identified with and succumbed to.

Friendship turned into flirtation almost overnight. It all started in our senior year of college, in separate bedrooms across town. We would both get stoned and talk to each other all night long on the phone. I would lie on my back on the sofa, staring up at the ceiling, sipping an Absolut cranberry, my head spinning and my dreams in perfect synchronization with the conversation. It felt like I was actually dreaming what I was doing. We would toy with the idea of simply kissing each other long before it ever happened.

I would tell her, "I have often thought about kissing a girl."

She would ask, "Does that excite you?"

And I would reply in a teasing, "Ye-es. I have thought about it every day and I am imagining it right now. And the girl is always you."

There would be a long pause in which I would take a sip of my drink, a long silence where I could hear nothing yet feel the beaming smile coming at me through the phone line from her side of town. She would say, in her soft melodic voice, "I have thought about you too." I would go to bed at night with a smile on my face, dreaming and fantasizing about what it would be like to actually do it. At that point no one I knew among my college friends had been with another woman and if they had, they sure didn't pipe up about it. I felt I would be different, a pioneer, and this thought gave me happiness and satisfaction. The same feeling I had from second grade returned; the mischievous desire to do something against the grain, to break a rule, had returned full force.

I vividly remember the night we finally acted on our desires.

Katie Moran

Kristina's father had given us a pair of his season tickets for the Great Western Forum near the airport. Before the Staples Center was built in downtown Los Angeles, the Forum was the place where the Kings hockey team played and all the good concerts would happen. We arrived at the stadium and realized that Celine Dion was singing that night. At the time I was not really familiar with her music so we sat in the parking lot most of the night while Kristina pounded beers. We went to the show for a while but the whole time I was thinking that the two of us could be doing something much more interesting, like taking each other's clothes off. I guess my wish was halfway granted when Kristina went behind someone's Volvo wagon, lifted up her skirt and peed on the asphalt. Not sexy. But if I didn't hold that type of behavior against a drunken guy, I wasn't going to hold it against a drunken girl.

We left the Forum and headed over to a guy friend's apartment in the marina. Being the good man that he was, he provided us with a cornucopia of drugs and alcohol and a bed to hang out in before starting a conversation about bisexuality. We admitted to him that we had thought about it. Kristina and I lay down on the bed next to each other; she looked at me with her adoring and knowing smile; I blushed. I turned over on my side lost in a daydream and when I turned back, Kristina had her shirt off, 36 DDs staring at me. She was wearing the most inviting and seductive expression I think I have ever seen. We kicked out our friend and I went for those tits with hands, eyes, lips, and tongue. It was empowering and just plain fucking hot. The combination of being turned on by a person and also by doing something considered wild or different was so intense that I hardly noticed the Rugby players walking in on us and pausing to take it all in.

The first time we had sex, about three weeks later, was pivotal; I thought about that first time for several weeks. I walked around campus in a complete daze. It was like living in a fantasy world. Because she was my best friend, we could talk about our sexual encounter the next day and evolve emotionally together. I felt like I had just stolen a million dollars and gotten away with it . . . yet there was no guilt. I had bottomed out on sex with men and this became my new drug of choice. I wanted to be with her all the time. The first time we had sex lasted for seven hours and the experience changed my view of sexuality and life forever. Some women talk about stuff and some women do it—Kristina and I were doers. We took action in every aspect of our lives, whether it be throwing the biggest party that other people could only imagine and talk about throwing, or jumping in the car to drive to the Mexican border, even if just for a good margarita.

The ups and downs of our relationship got to be too extreme. We would have great nights together yet the next morning I would wake up to find out she was having sex with another partner. Some of Kristina's more unsavory choices were, not necessarily in this order: my younger brother in my hot tub while I slept inside the house, my boss in another hot tub in the Hollywood Hills, and, of course, random college boys willing to eat pussy. The most hurtful was a girl she met on a business trip to New York. We were each other's first girls so when she added a second female I felt left out and left behind. Kristina was a drunk and her decisions proved it. She had a problem with kissing another woman in public but had no qualms about having sex with three men in one night. I am a very forgiving person, so because of the intense love between us, and because of the lack of defined boundaries, our relationship continued.

One day I was walking my dog along the pier in Hermosa Beach when I saw Kristina hanging off the balcony of her favorite bar, drinking out of a sangria pitcher, two straws stuck in her mouth. She saw me, waved, and welcomed me with open arms. Another friend ran up to us and shouted, "Hey, come to my party on Fifth right after the bar closes!" I was not dressed

Katie Moran

for a party but couldn't pass up the opportunity for a DJ and free drinks. Of course, this meant my dog would be coming too. At the house everyone was on ecstasy and became fascinated with the soft texture of my dog's fur. The dog tolerated all the stroking for a little while, but finally I realized she was a bit spooked by all the attention and I had to push them off. Kristina stumbled out of a bedroom in search of me, pointing an accusatory finger as if I had been escaping her grasp all evening. She stuck her hand in the back pocket of my jeans and pulled me down the hall toward the bedroom, explaining that there were some people who wanted to have an orgy and she did not want to do it without me.

I was sober and had never had sex with strangers before, especially not a multitude of them, and I was not interested, but after a forceful and passionate kiss in the hallway, Kristina convinced me to join them. As I followed Kristina, the line for the bathroom cheered; they had witnessed our kiss and agreed I should go with her! I entered the room to find a bed with two nice-looking young guys and one very hot LeAnn Rhimes look-alike by the name of, coincidentally, Lee.

The night turned out to be a blast. All five of us fit nicely on the queen-sized bed and the two men were kind enough to make my dog a bed out of jackets and sweatshirts so that she could sleep in the corner. My pet peeve is a guy who is too insecure to have sex in front of a dog, so these guys went up on my list as acceptable partners. After all, the dog sleeps and pays no interest to what people are doing in bed so what does it matter? It isn't like they are impressionable young children. These guys were cute. And cute nice guys who liked dogs equaled sex. I know, my standards were really high. Lee was the second girl I was with and she differed enormously from Kristina. She was very feminine yet aggressive in bed.

Kristina was a "layback girl," a woman who just lays on her back waiting for penetration or for her partner to do ALL the work; because of that, sex with Kristina had grown very one-sided so the way Lee took charge was a welcome change. I think experiencing reciprocity in bed at the orgy marked the beginning of the end for Kristina and me. The orgy ended with Lee and Kristina giving the two guys blowjobs, sparing me from the task.

I woke up the next morning and Lee and one of the guys were gone. My dog was still sleeping peacefully on the pile of garments. Kristina was asleep next to me and so was the other guy whose bed we were in. Suddenly there was a knock and the door swung open. Standing in the doorway was a man in an orange shirt and matching cap . . . the cable guy! I hate those kinds of wake-up calls. He was in shock at what he saw, two naked girls lying in bed with one naked guy and a fiercely barking dog.

My birthday falls on National Coming Out Day but I never officially came out to anyone as straight or gay or anything in between. My best friend called me on my eighteenth birthday and left a message. I called her back and she said, "I'm gay." And I said, "That's great, I figured that out when you were six. Aren't you going to wish me a happy birthday?"

I was always honest with my friends about being with women and if they were offended by my sexuality then they weren't my friends anymore. I lost two friends who said they were okay with it to my face but then expressed disgust to other people and ultimately could not handle it. My mom found out quite by accident because my brother told her. She was not happy about it but now says that our relationship as mother and daughter transcends anything else. I think it might have been something she picked up in therapy.

There are some members of my family who know the extent of my sexuality and some that know nothing. With an Italian family of over a hundred members, there are people you are close to and those that you only see at weddings and funerals.

Katie Moran

My grandparents still try to fix me up with anyone with a penis under the age of forty-five who comes near their house, whether it is a contractor, a real estate agent, or the deadbeat son of one of their bridge mates. You would think they would have realized that I am not the straightest of kids when I showed up to their 50th wedding anniversary party with Kristina, got drunk, and danced half the night with my head passed out on her shoulder. My grandfather has offered me $10,000 to have his first great-grandchild. I jokingly asked him if I could use the money for in-vitro fertilization but he said that method did not count. Out of his ten grandchildren, I doubt I will be the first to have a baby. Even before being with a woman, I always considered adopting a child. My dog was an unwanted soul who found her way to me; some of the best things in life come from things other than oneself.

If you have any inkling that you want to be with a member of the same sex, even if just for one night, do it. It is like losing your virginity all over again, at least it was for me. I suppose the official term for someone like me would be "bisexual"; there are some days when all I want is a good-looking Stetson model to come home to, and other days I just want to crawl into a woman's embrace and hide. It has been seven years since my first time with a woman and I have been with seven more since then. No two encounters are the same. Kristina and I kept our affair going for over two years, finally saying the words "I love you" after a good amount of time before slowly fading out of each other's lives.

We both saw many boyfriends come and go but we always remained together. It was our secret, for the most part. I only told the men I was dating the truth about my relationship with Kristina but she kept it completely in the closet. I think she wanted a long-term relationship with a man, to get married and have children, and did not want her affairs with women to jeopardize her lifelong goals. This hurt me. I secretly wanted her to love me enough to not want anyone else. But a big part of me hung on to the straight world despite how strongly I felt about her as a person, as a companion. In fact, my relationships with both Austin and Kristina slightly overlapped. Remember, she was the one who introduced us that night at the bar.

Unlike Kristina, I was nowhere near ready for a serious relationship with a man so I lacked any fear of their opinions of me. I treated most men as objects of desire, to be used for my pleasure and then disposed of at whim. The majority of the time, it was mutual. Men in their early twenties, especially LA guys, are usually not looking for anything more serious than a fuck. It was rare in those days for me to care if a relationship ended; I believed I could quickly and painlessly find another guy to replace the one I had been with.

I met Kristina about a year ago for a lunch on Canon Drive; it was the first time I had seen her in three years. She was seeing a man that she was in love with and intended to marry; I was single and very happy. As we talked I realized that some people never change; she looked great and was still finishing my sentences. Kristina had aged a bit and was still drinking excessively but it did not affect her overall appeal. She knew me so well and could still make me feel right at home. But I guess that is what best friends do. To me, that is what is so special about being with a woman. It is the friendship, the camaraderie and the comfort. I have not found the same feeling with men but I know other women who have. My friend Mia's boyfriend is the sweetest guy on planet Earth. She says that being with him is like being with her best friend, other than having to watch football and listen to him play video games.

My experiences with women continued after Kristina. I remained fascinated by the same sex until women became less of a novelty and more of just another option, a way of life. I have been with an array of beautiful girls including a Miss Hawaiian

Tropic and a gorgeous actress whom I fell in love with but left because I could sense that she was not okay with the whole thing. After two years we became great friends, as women often do become despite the strangest of circumstances. Then there was Jasmine, a twenty-one-year-old model who totally blew my skirt up. She was into large-sized dildos and mild beatings, among other things. Jasmine had an affinity for drinking too much, driving her huge Mercedes over to my place, parking it, and stumbling up the Spanish steps of my house and knocking rudely at 3 AM. Her behavior was completely offensive at times, yet she was still too beautiful to turn away, even with hot dog relish all over her mouth.

But, as I continued on with my escapades, I began longing for something more. I wanted something—or rather someone— real for a change. I did a lot of talking. If men and women are exactly the same, if their souls do not differ, are we all able to fall in love with anyone of either sex? "Are people just people?" For most people there are too many other factors such as phys- ical attraction, social implications, and some deeper inexplica- ble spiritual connections that determine attraction. Being bisexual means that you do not discriminate. The goal is to love and be loved in return, to find another human being of either sex to make love to and spend time with. Many bisexual women are different; some just want a little girl-on-the-side action, a sexy secret to share with their boyfriends. A much smaller percentage of bisexual women are mostly gay, but oc- casionally have sex with men. Many bisexual women stay away from any emotional entanglements altogether and some are just "curious"; they never take it too far. And then some are like me—real bisexual women who go fifty-fifty. In the spirit of James Dean, I just want to be happy—and you can't do that with one hand tied behind your back.

4

The One-Night Stand

I am not a man. I don't know what men think. I suspect, however, that the majority of men would not mind getting laid after a night out. I would even say that a lot of men go to a bar or a club to pick up a woman to have sex with. Men also browse personals sites on the Internet, possibly to meet women to have sex with. Women do it too. Of course, there are those women, the majority of my single friends, who get all bitched out to ho-themselves on a nightly manhunt . . . the ever-popular boyfriend search.

One of my favorite phrases, taught to me by my gay friends, is "trolling for cock." Recently, a friend of mine and I went to a comedy show on Sunset. After the show ended my friend insisted that we stand by the exit of the club to try to meet the headlining act, a very good-looking and hilariously funny

Canadian guy. In his act he said that it is obvious when a woman wants to sleep with you if they sit on your bed. After thinking about this for a minute I realized he was absolutely right. When my friend and I arrived at the exit, there were ten or so other women all waiting for the comedian to walk out. They were anxiously peering up over the backs of each other's heads, fixing their hair, and putting out their cigarettes. This is what can only be described as "trolling for cock."

This particular guy had some major sex appeal. Even my most prudish friend admitted that she would have a one-night stand with him. When the comedian appeared, the competition was fierce. I stood back and admired the scene. One girl screamed out, "I will sit on your bed anytime!" The man ducked his head down and escaped the crowd, leaving my friend and the other girls disappointed. It has been my experience that those who seek rarely find. Going out should be about just that—getting out of the house to have fun and spend time with friends, let loose, see a show, or maybe dance a little . . . or a lot.

One night, I went out with my friend who was visiting for the weekend. Talia, a thirty-five-year-old divorcée and business manager for Las Vegas casino owners and restaurateurs, was looking for a new man. After discovering that Sky Bar was full of nothing but aging, foreign men claiming to be producers, and that the Four Seasons lobby harbored more prostitutes than the Chicken Ranch in Nevada, we ended up bar hopping all over town. We'd walk in, Talia would scope the place for bachelors and then force us to leave if there was no one available. I would be halfway through a martini when she would abruptly yank my arm and say, "Get your purse. Only baldies and fatties here."

There are other women who, just like the stereotypical male, go out with the sex agenda in mind. After my break-up with Austin, I was all about getting laid. I wanted to find some nameless specimen and make him mine for one night only. I like the idea of one-night stands; in fact, I think they are very underrated. Gay men have grasped this concept and taken it full throttle. Straight women call it a fling; gay men call it fucking.

My friend Bobby can go out to a bar, meet someone ten times hotter than any straight guy out there, have sex, and be back at the bar in time for last call. I wish I could remember half the one-night stands that I have had, but I was usually drunk, and that is not a recommendation. Some one-night stands are what I call accidental one-nighters. This is when a woman sleeps with a man that she is dating or intending on sleeping with again, but the sex is bad, and she does not repeat it. Sometimes the accidental one-nighter can happen in reverse. Someone sleeps with you and decides not to go back for seconds. Sometimes it's no one's fault, just a non-committal partner or someone who only wanted sex in the first place and knows that it is getting too serious. Other times, a woman has a problem that keeps guys from returning to the box.

Take Anna, a writer, who sleeps with plenty of men, but not by choice. She wishes one of them would stick around, she'd love to be someone's girlfriend. Anna always wonders why men inevitably leave her after she sleeps with them. According to her they could be going out for two months but the moment they sleep together, he bails on her. I was fascinated by this and decided to do some digging, so when one of the guys from her past began dating one of my friends, I asked him the reason. He laughed and he said, "Oh, who Anna? You mean, tackle box? Stinky puss? When I pulled off those panties I knew it was over." Ouch! I could not decide who I felt worse for, Anna, because she was unaware of her hygiene problem, or all the men who had to suffer through a night with her. From what I have heard, the problem still remains. I am guessing no one has told her that her pussy stinks. My advice to her is, obviously, to

Katie Moran

wash and put some powder on that thing or find a man who has lost his sense of smell in an accident.

As far as one-night stands, give it a try—safely—if you have not already. Look your best and go to a place where you feel the most comfortable, free, and in your own element. For instance, if you like musicians, go see a live band play at a small, packed club. If you are into the executive BMW-driving type, try a swanky hotel bar. If you drink too much and can handle emotionally needy men, go to an AA meeting. It's about the easiest thing to do . . . almost all men are game. Just make sure you have sex on your mind when you approach them and it will shine right through in your eyes. Make your move with intention. It's as easy as saying, "Want to go back to my place?"

My favorite one–night stand was a nameless blue-eyed Moroccan. I am sure he told me his name; I think he even gave me his number, but I promptly forgot it. I left all of my friends on the dance floor, some disgusted by my behavior, some worried for my safety, and took him home from the club in a cab (we both had cars but it was far more adventurous this way). I chose him because he was gorgeous, and we just had this lucid connection on a very primal level. The air between us was balmy and thick and I was in the mood to have a good time (four shots of tequila sometimes has that effect on me). I was turned on by the sense of urgency, the quick trip to the corner store for condoms, the groping in the backseat of the cab, and the keys left in the door while we tore each other's clothes off without even making it to the bedroom.

I actually preferred having sex with this stranger on the couch—kind of hypocritical, I know. He was good enough for me to ride for an hour but not good enough to see the inside of my bedroom and dirty the nice sheets. After we had our fun, we went back to the club and I joined my friends as if nothing happened. I forgot one small detail: some men actually have feelings. This one was particularly sensitive and wanted to validate the experience by exchanging phone numbers, names, blah, blah, yawn. No, no, and an emphatic no. I thanked him for a great time but told him, "Let's not ruin a perfectly nice evening with formalities."

Men need to be objectified and treated like pieces of meat on occasion. This is not permission to be a vicious human being, but sometimes you have to wonder why it's okay for a man to sleep with countless women but not the reverse. The only way to turn this around is to even the score. Feel free to add another name to your list of lovers. Maybe it will be the one who makes you smile every time you think back on the experience. Being a slut is only a state of mind anyway, because you are the only one who has to wake up with yourself the next morning. Only you know what behavior is acceptable to you. If it worries you too much, practice the "behind closed doors" phenomenon and keep your activities to yourself. They don't call it a "personal" life for no reason.

Bobby had not had sex in quite a while; a big problem for a gay man whose identity was based on whom he was sleeping with. Like the rest of West Hollywood, he had recently become hooked on dating Web sites like Match.com, MySpace, and Friendster. After three days of searching the men-interested-in-dating-other-men section, Bobby had more emails from fine-looking guys than I had received all year. Of course, it helped that we had Photoshopped his Friendster account photo to look like he had been lifting weights every day for a year and had an ass that was so high it almost reached his neck. He had Friendster emails from Derek, Dwayne, Brad, Johnston (yes, that is a real gay man's name), Kyle, Kendrick, and Jude, just to name a few.

One Friday night Bobby invited me over to his house to have dinner with him. However, instead of eating I was playing with his dog by myself for two hours in the living room while he sat on the computer like a crack addict, eyes glued to the screen. I

Katie Moran

offered him coffee and he actually shooed me aside. Finally at one o'clock in the morning I told Bobby I was going to leave and he said, "No, need wardrobe advice." He had a date to have sex with some twenty-year-old law student in Malibu. I helped him pick out a proper one-night-stand outfit, a pair of Diesel jeans and a Puma T-shirt, all the while thinking to myself that a more accurate name for Friendster would be "Fuckster." While my straight friends have little luck with online dating, the gay guys I know who use it are hopping across town at all hours having sex with strangers. For Bobby getting laid was as easy as turning on a radio; straight men have to work a little harder. We walked out the door of his apartment off Santa Monica Boulevard, and I yelled, "Wear a condom!" as he got into his car. He backed out of the driveway, put the car in drive, rolled down the window, and said, "I'm a bottom!" getting looks of horror from two women walking to their car from a nearby bar . . .

The next morning Bobby called me to tell me how the date went. I asked him, "Was he hot? Was the sex any good?" Bobby sounded dreamy as he replied, "I am so in love. He is the perfect guy. We talked all night long and just held each other. Then I gave him a massage." Bobby's excitement surprised me; I thought for sure his "date" was a one-night stand in the making. Bobby called Mr. Perfect the next day and left him a message, inviting him to an erotic VIP party with free drinks, go-go dancers, and a buffet. The guy never called him back. I felt horrible for Bobby; he was crushed. He dragged me along to the party instead, chain smoking Salems, and sipping his Pellegrino angrily, staring down any queen that looked his way as if to say, "You stole him from me, didn't you bitch?"

I told Bobby that he would be fine; that you never know what you will find on the Internet. But it was hard for him not to take it personally. Like all of us, he thought if only he was better looking or smarter or said one thing instead of another that it would have made some sort of difference. The fact is you cannot make someone love you, and it's not your fault if they don't. Everybody likes to think that they are powerful and can control certain situations but ultimately we can't make other people think or feel what we would like them to. As I explained my hard-earned lessons to Bobby he glared at me, straw jammed into his mouth, sucking away, and mumbled, "It was a one-night stand up. Fuck Friendster." But later on that night, he was back to browsing.

A traditional one-night stand can be very freeing. The kind of one-nighter when someone really attracts your attention and something inside of you tells you to go for it and you do, and it is great. But one-night stands can also suck . . . big time. In fact, the majority of them do. But not because of the cheap and tawdry stigma placed on them; it is the physical implications of trying to physically mesh with a stranger that can make one-night stands unfulfilling. First, you are dealing with a mystery penis (or clitoris . . . whatever you prefer). Unzip, and God knows what will be revealed; it can be very disappointing. The fact that there is no emotional connection with the person can either be an incredible turn-on or it can leave you feeling a little empty and freaked out. Try it one time (or a few dozen times) and see. You'll know.

One evening in particular stands out in my memory for its unique combination of chance and circumstance that caused two very different people to come together creating that magical, if only momentary, friction. In this case it was more than chemistry, it was a collision between two high-voltage people that caused sparks so big you could almost see them and most definitely feel them, even if only witnessing it from afar. The air has to be right, ideally one of those calm and breezy evenings that feel like the tropics even when cars are whizzing by and the DJ is playing Britney Spears while people are breaking beer bottles all around you. It was a bit like Olivia Newton-John and

Katie Moran

John Travolta singing "Summer Nights" in *Grease* except, in my case, it was November.

This particular evening my friend Nicolas was DJ-ing at a gay bar in Hollywood, and I decided to go visit him there and maybe see a few other friends. I certainly was not going with the intention of meeting anyone except fabulous drag queens that could show me how to properly blend two separate shades of lipstick into one alluring color, or, the preferred drag queen spelling, "colour." After fixing my lip colour, I ran into the bar owner who gave me two drink tickets and lifted me up in the air as his hello. He was so hot, I thought. Too bad he is gay! Then, through the crowd of Dolces, Gabbanas, cabin-boys, and barflies, I saw her. She caught the corner of my eye and I focused in like I was looking at her through a telescope. Everything else fell away and this woman was all I saw.

Now up until this point, the only women I had dated were "girls," young model chicks in their early twenties just coming into their sexuality, far more focused on getting drunk or getting high and experiencing everything on overload. Laura was a woman, and I knew it the first time I saw her sitting at the bar with her friends. I walked right up to her without any hesitation or self-doubt and fed her a line that I knew would work, just as it worked for Bobby the week before. "Where have you been hiding? I have been calling and calling you all day."

She replied, "I would have tried to find you but I don't have your number. And let's not start this again, we're here now aren't we?"

I nodded.

"Then what would you like to drink?" she asked.

"Anything you're having," I answered.

She descended on me, responding, "Oh, no, we'll have none of that. What would *you* like to drink?"

I said, "What you're having, a Corona."

And so it was. She immediately put her arm around me and I

could smell the Coco Chanel fragrance mingling with the alcohol. In retrospect I should have realized that there was a possibility she was already drunk but the thought never crossed my mind.

After I finished my beer, Laura dragged me off my barstool and I got to see all five foot ten of her thin model-like frame. She had a face exactly like Michelle Pfeiffer's only more beautiful, if that is even possible. She yanked me toward the back of the bar, dragging me past Nicolas who looked up from his spinning in amazement and gave me a quick thumbs up and a nod that only I could see as we whizzed by at warp speed. My legs could barely keep up with her runway strides. She cornered me in the bathroom and locked the door. I surprised her by flipping her around and pushing her against the wall, kissing her. She told me it was the best kiss she had ever had in her life. The heat was so intense as angry people with bladders full of liquor banged on the door and yelled at us to wrap it up. She stared deep into my soul and I pounced back. She looked as if she was about to cry. It was a scene out of an '80s movie.

The rest of the evening grew even more passionate. We went back to her friends' place where she was staying. Laura explained she was only in town for a month on vacation from her job as a producer in South Africa. Her friends were amazed by Laura's behavior, one of them, a very straight girl named Natalie with curly hair and a startled look in her eyes, kept glancing at us and saying, "I am a nice Jewish girl, what is going on here, Laura?!" Laura, I loved the name Laura. I am sure I would have loved the name Percy if that were her name instead. I was twenty-four and she was thirty-seven, the oldest person I had ever had any sexual contact with, although to me she looked like she was twenty-seven. It was certainly the most intense intimacy I had experienced with someone I had just met. The connection was so strong she had tears in her eyes.

Katie Moran

That night I had been at the bar with my dog, Soda. Soda had gotten used to accompanying me to bars or waiting anxiously in the car during her puppy-hood. If I left her alone at home she would pee and poo everywhere, eat a sofa or two and generally just piss off my roommate. Soda was with me that night and took a liking to Laura but by 3 AM Soda had overstayed her welcome at Laura's friend's house. Besides, Laura and I needed some serious space and privacy. I took both of my ladies back to my place a short distance down the same street.

In the sky was a full Gemini moon and Laura was Gemini. It felt as if some overwhelming force in the atmosphere was literally pushing us together. We had sex against the washing machine, on the kitchen table, in my shower, on the bathroom floor, and in my bed. We clung to each other and said we were falling in love, made promises never to hurt each other, to gain trust and to stay together forever. We felt safe in each other's arms. Soda was not used to sharing a bed with another woman but she slept on top of Laura all night. No one liked Soda, so it really touched me that Laura did not push her to the floor. During out night together I never once thought about how ridiculous this "insta-love" was. I have lived in many dream worlds because I have a tendency to let my fantasies become my realities—but in this case, it did seem that the two worlds were joining as one.

We talked about everything that night. We talked about how she was adopted, was an only child, and feared being unwanted by even her adopted mother. This should have been a red flag that she required an insane amount of emotional attention. But I fell deeper into the fantasy. I was going to be the one to save her from this life of sadness, I decided at that moment. She had never been married but wanted so desperately to be loved and I told her that I was that person. She explained how she had horrible luck with men. Then we casually mentioned our private educations, not to brag but to prove that we measured up and equaled each other's high standards of excellence. I was a twenty-four-year-old, barely-working writer and she, a well-established but emotionally unstable television producer living in another country. Yeah, it was the perfect match.

We discussed how Laura had not been with a woman for a few years but that something inside her was telling her that she should be with a woman. The word "lesbian" intimidated her, but then what straight girl isn't freaked out by it? We talked about the stereotypes of dykes with cheap haircuts and economical SUVs like Rav-4s or Honda CR-Vs and all those other expressions of lesbian bad taste like unibrows or inverted mouths. Laura had full lips and was very feminine. I am not attracted to girls that look like boys, only girls that look like girls, girly girls. I like shoes-that-match-the-handbag type of girls and Laura fit the criteria; she was Fendi all the way. She invited me to move to South Africa and live with her, saying that she could never be without me. She cried and said she knew she could trust me. Then we took a shower together. This was a bad scene from a soft-core porno! Yet I fell for it.

I woke up in the morning having no regrets, and saw her still looking as beautiful as ever lying on the pillow next to me sleeping, the back of her neck still lightly scented with Coco Chanel. Though I am a very passionate person, I still retain a little bit of level-headedness. I rely on my instincts and they are rarely wrong, so I was convinced of the accuracy of feeling that Laura and I were meant to be after that first encounter. I took it as a sign that Soda did not shit six times on the floor in protest of me sleeping with Laura. I dated one guy for four months and every time he came over, my dog gave him the evil eye and then eked out as many poops as she could on my living room floor. She liked Laura and I took this to mean more than it actually did, which is that Soda just likes women more than men or

Katie Moran

takes to anyone that likes her over someone who ignores her. My imagination was on overload.

Bobby came by my house at noon to take me to brunch at Swingers on Beverly where we ate every Saturday because of their great French toast and patio full of eye candy. When Laura came out of the bedroom Bobby took one look at her and raised a plucked eyebrow in complete admiration. I could barely hide the smile. I looked like I had just caught the biggest fish at the lake or won a teddy bear at a fair. We drove Laura back to her friend's house and she promised that she would take a shower and call me. In fact she said it twice, "I'll call you." She was going to join Bobby and me for brunch and shopping; it was the first day of the rest of our lives. I even changed the sheets and rolled a lint brush over my velvet duvet cover because I knew she would be back that evening.

Though I knew it was too early to use the term "soul mate" I still felt that there was something that fused my heart to her on that very first night we met. Something cosmic and unexplainable, and I almost always have an answer for everything. But that was all it turned out to be. One night. The only night. Even as we made our plans to meet again in a few hours Laura knew our evening was just another one-night stand. She never called me. Our last kiss in the car was the big kiss off.

I left messages that she never returned. I stared helplessly at the business card with all her numbers on it, her e-mail address, and her office location in South Africa. I felt crushed. Even worse than the heartbreak was realizing I had never been so wrong about anything in my life. My instincts had failed me. I have had sex with numerous partners, many just once or twice, and I always knew when there would be no phone call, and never really cared. It was just a mutual thing with the person I was having sex with. I had an instinct that told me "This is just sex" or "This is a future relationship." Some flings would start with fire then fizzle out in a few weeks, but that first phone call after a long and emotional night was inevitable, expected, and most of all, valued.

Laura was the only woman I had ever slept with who was more than two years older than I was. All of my other lovers had been in their early twenties. And they all called the next day . . . every single one of them. If a guy did not call me the next day after sex, he was immediately out of the picture and there were no regrets. But they all called the next day, except one poor guy who got reamed by my best friend for calling me two days later instead of right away. Poor guy thought I was busy. As for the girls, I have known all of them for years and never lost touch with an ex-lover of the female gender. I thought that a real woman, a thirty-seven-year-old perfect example of femininity and womanhood, would have at least had the decency to call and explain.

Sometimes all we want is an explanation. But no one is perfect and life is full of surprises. I may never know why she was unable or unwilling to see me again. I missed her for a long time after that. Bobby would take me on drive-bys of the house where she was staying to see if she was still there. Yes, I had resorted to stalking. After only a few days I felt like a part of me had been flattened and pulled out. I suspect it was because it was more than just a physical fuck. It was a mind fuck.

I was freshly fucked over and it took months to shake that feeling. I was shocked at how strongly I felt for Laura but knew in my heart that sometimes it is best to let the emotions run their course and not to try to force one's own feelings to heal quickly. I wish Laura were here right now because I have so many questions for her. I would ask her what her life is like today and why she was so scared off on that fateful day. My dog Soda feared that she would never meet someone (other than me) that is so tolerant of her. She was wrong, because Laura did teach me one valuable lesson: Respect my dog and I

Katie Moran

will respect you. If someone you are dating is disrespectful of your pets, your children, or your family, then you should not be with them. Respect for those three things is showing that they have respect for you. And we should have that same respect for the people we date when it comes to those aforementioned groups. My dog communicates very well, obviously. Either that or I got so bored waiting for Laura to call back that I made up dialogue for my dog and I to have. But I hope that Laura one day realizes that losing her was, for me, a day as bad as the night before had been good.

Some of the best times in life are not planned. I never planned on going up to a strange girl at a bar one November night, but being open and aware creates a life that is so above the ordinary that it feels like I am operating on a different plane. That is why one day I realized that I was done with one-night stands and that I had grown out of them for the time being. I was twenty-five and met a guy named Page through a friend's band. We had sex and the condom was so dry that it actually turned into a bubble on this guy's dick. The thrusting motion had created a valve that acted like a little pump and with each stroke this pocket of air grew bigger and bigger until the whole condom had turned into a big, distended bubble. Needless to say, the sex sucked. We threw the condom on the ground and went to sleep. In the middle of the night I was awoken by this weird rubbery churning type sound. I looked down to see Soda staring up at me cross-eyed furiously chewing, a tiny circle sticking out of her mouth. I pulled the circle out (which was a strain as she was really holding on to this thing) and out slid our used condom. She has had a ton of other unmentionables in her mouth but this knotted condom was one of the worst.

As disgusting as it was, I was totally cracking up and went to wake up Page and tell him about it. As I reached out to shake him I realized that I didn't even know this guy well enough to wake him up; he probably wouldn't even find it funny. That is when I realized that I wanted more out of my sex life. I had had my fair share of fun and great experiences but this night with Page made me realize that when the sex came without even friendship there was something lacking.

It has been a while since my last one-night stand and I would consider another fling if the right person came along. I have set one goal in regards to future one-night stands: If there can't be emotion, at least it can serve to win me points in the game I play with a few friends. Basically, we make a short list of all the famous people we want to have sex with and see who can get the closest. One friend beat me to it by having sex with the guitarist of a very famous rock band. I guess even without friendship one-night stands still have their place.

The drawbacks of one-night stands are plentiful. The most serious side effect of a one-night stand is human emotion. I never once thought that I would get my feelings hurt by having a one-nighter. As women, we often forget that we feel—but everyone feels. I have hurt men by not wanting to see them again after a one-night stand but at least now I call and give them an explanation because I know that there is nothing worse than an unreturned phone call. On the flip side, there are some exciting possibilities when it comes to one-nighters. My friend and her husband started their relationship with a drunken one-nighter at a beach party. One-night stands can also open people up to a world of sexual exploration they never knew was out there. People can reveal their darkest fantasies, try all kinds of new tricks, and scream out such indecencies as, "Put your finger in my ass like you mean it!" or "You will never be fucked this good again!" without wondering, "Will he call me tomorrow?"

There is a certain liberation in knowing a person may always remember you as a freak, but you'll never have to see him again. Women are used all the time for sex, so there is no reason why men shouldn't be. Be polite, but throw them out like four-day-old pizza when you are through. Most men will not even hate you for it, because hey, they got laid . . . and so did you.

5

Explaining, Searching, and Finding

How many times have we all heard the words, "So, are you seeing anyone?" The mind races, the explaining begins, the stories of failed relationships, the way-too-busy career, and the non-committal guy you are dating on and off spill pathetically from your mouth. And what is this whole business of "finding" someone? Like a man is a pearl in an oyster somewhere? "Oh, check it out, Kelly, I found this multi-millionaire husband underneath the hood of an old Subaru. Don't touch him; he's mine. I found him first!"

One of my favorite movie scenes is in *Four Weddings and a Funeral* when, at a wedding, an older woman asks a younger woman, "Are you married?" When she replies, "No," the older woman follows it with, "Are you a lesbian?" The young woman is startled and again says no. The older woman continues, "Well, it is far more interesting than, 'Just haven't found the right chap?'"

My mom used to ask me all the time, "But what was wrong with this one? He seemed nice." I would get so tired of explaining, yet again, that it doesn't matter how nice the guy is, sometimes it just doesn't work. Sometimes relationships stop working and it is no one's fault and no one needs to feel bad about it. So, instead of explaining that he had no goals in life or that I liked being with my friends more than him or one of those other incidental reasons that aren't really the real reasons why people break up; I lied: "Mom, he liked to dress up in my underwear, fuck my roommate and then molest her pet fish, steal my car and go to glory holes in Fresno." My mother, who has a great sense of humor replied, "Well, that's not so bad, at least he didn't fuck your sister!"

With the rest of my family, it is not so easy. I come from a very large Italian family. When all of us are in the same room at the same time, the noise is so loud all that can be heard is an ear-deafening buzz. There are dozens of strong personalities fighting to keep up with each other. In a family like that, you either rise to the occasion or drown from the pressure. My family does not need to say anything about me not being married anymore. Their scornful looks speak volumes. They used to tell me, "You're young, you have plenty of time!" Now, in my late-twenties they just shake their heads and assume the worst.

There are powerful societal pressures to be partnered up and married away. My parents and grandparents are no longer waiting on the edges of their seats for my wedding day, but the fact that so many of my friends are getting married and doing couple things sometimes makes me think I should do it, too. Yes, I too am a victim of couple peer pressure. However, the real pressure usually comes from the woman herself. The need

The "On" Position

to find someone—that craving or need for companionship—is most often self-inflicted. I often hear my single girlfriends complain, "How did she land that guy? I am better looking than she is. He must like bimbos that don't challenge him." (Long pause and then a sob.) "But what the fuck is wrong with *me?*"

It's hard to avoid the over-abundance of explanations and rationalizations people give when asked about relationships. A friend of mine tried to set me up with this recently divorced guy. It was just supposed to be a friendly meeting on a work project; it wasn't even a date at this point. When he asked me if I was seeing anyone, I simply said "No." It was not necessary for me to explain that I still had my ex-boyfriend's stuff at my place and that even though in my mind I was single and the relationship was done it was possible my ex wasn't as clear on that as I was. If I wanted to date the new guy and felt strongly enough about him, I would definitely be able to clear out the ex's stuff. So I felt it was a better choice to withhold unnecessary information than bring all that baggage in on a first meeting.

After I told him that I was single, he offered up the fact that he had been married for nine years; that his wife was not exactly his type, that he preferred women who did this more and that less . . . and for the next ten minutes all this useless information came spilling out of his mouth like vomit. I appreciated his honesty about his ex but the torrent of explanations was a turn-off; they only made me realize that I was the wrong girl for him. When he continued to pursue me, again explaining that he was sentimentally attached to his ten-year-old-sorry-ass-broken-down car and that he needed me to pick him up just this once, I basically tuned him out completely. Explanations take all of the mystery out of dating. And over-explaining can paint a pathetic portrait of who someone really is. On the other hand, it is good to know a person's offensive characteristics right off the bat so you know they are wrong for you.

Katie Moran

My friend Jasmine can sense when a guy does not want to hear about it. What is "it"? Well, "it" is T.M.I., or "too much information." Jasmine had been involved with this man for ten years on and off. He was in love with her in high school when they were both fourteen but she never gave him the time of day. She spent several years becoming used to the fact that he worshipped her. His constant devotion was a staple in her life. She would walk out of class and find roses on her car. This continued all the way through college. Then, when it stopped and she re-examined the situation a few years later she asked herself, "What have I done? Have I let go of a good thing?"

Suddenly, after all these years the tables were turned and she was desperately in love with this guy. She wrote him letters that she never delivered to him and even cried at the thought of them not being together. At the wedding of his brother, he had too much to drink and asked for her hand in marriage. He climbed up on a chair and announced to the crowd of about 200 people that he was in love with her and wanted to have children with her. She thought she was going to have a heart attack; this was exactly what she wanted to hear.

Unfortunately, Jasmine was involved in an unhealthy relationship with another man at the time. This guy was a typical gangster; he was involved in insurance fraud and was just an all around scamster. He had weaseled tens of thousands out of Jasmine and destroyed her credit. Jasmine longed to regain the innocence she had with the boy who left flowers on her car all those years ago. When they finally had a chance to be alone in a hotel room after the wedding was over, Jasmine decided to tell her high school sweetheart how she felt about him. Her new-found emotions did not put him off but what did was her explanation of the bad relationship with the con-artist boyfriend.

As she was talking, she could see his eyes glass over and his gaze grow distant. She said she was trying to explain her bad decisions away to show that she was not the one to blame and to get out of being at fault for the financial problems. She was trying to paint herself as a victim, which was not an attractive portrait. She thought that by admitting to her weaknesses she would show that she trusted this guy from her past with her heart. Instead, he was put off by her poor judgment and was scared of crossing lines with her. He cared about her and decided that she needed time to heal and find herself after this detrimental relationship. In essence, he gave her his pity and that was the last thing she wanted. She had explained herself right out of a potential relationship. She realized, many months and even many more unreturned phone calls later, that some things have to be kept on a "need to know" basis.

Recently this sexy young guy asked me for a date. His line was, "What's your story?" When someone asks me to tell a story, writer mode kicks in. As I was telling him about myself, over-informing him, I could see his attraction slowly shut down and turn off. It was really interesting to watch his initial interest in me turn to borderline disgust. I am very honest and matter-of-fact about my life and who I am and sometimes it puts people off. Maybe that is a good thing; perhaps it is better to scare off men who cannot handle a strong personality. Or maybe I am overdosing Mr. Right with too much me up front. I should leave some surprises waiting in the wings; a girl has to have some tricks up her sleeve!

Women sometimes feel the need to explain why they are not in a relationship as if it is some sort of disease to be single. Like, "Oh, I am not married but I think it will clear up soon if I see a doctor and do this and follow these instructions and stop working so much and reduce my stress . . ." The reasons to stay single are not a mystery—I think some people who stay married have more explaining to do! There are as many good reasons to be single as there are to be married. Making the commitment to get married requires love, compatibility, and

Katie Moran

conviction. When my friend Mariah was asked by another woman, "Are you seeing anyone?" She replied, "I'm married." And that statement ended the conversation. When this woman turned her attention to our other friend Nicole, Nicole lied and said, "I'm married, too," because she really did not want to explain her single-hood.

So many people seem to want an explanation of your personal life and sometimes the inquisition extends beyond just making good conversation. One man at a party asked me what my "sexual preference" was and I just chose not to answer the question at all. I almost laughed out loud. Only I know that "sexual" preference has little to do with my overall attraction to a person. A few years ago I would have spent ten minutes discussing with this stranger my views on attraction and my past with women and men, sex and emotions, intellect and interests. Now, I flatly asked this man, "What's your preference?" He looked at me with disdain, as if what I said was a complete insult to his manhood. He replied, "I'm straight, can't you tell?" I was thinking, "Yeah, you are definitely straight. You're not cute or funny and no gay man would be seen out wearing those tired shoes!"

There came a point when I just stopped explaining my personal life altogether. I have found that explaining too much about my past can be damaging to a new relationship. A significant other is a subjective being with different opinions and judgments who will ultimately hold a different opinion of my behavior than I do. For instance, I have had sex with a friend or two on occasion just for fun but I still do not consider myself promiscuous. When I shared this with a person I had just begun dating, a guy who had slept with far fewer people than I have, he considered my behavior a deviation from what is acceptable. After making the decision to not place judgments on my sexual behavior and standing behind my decisions on what I do physically, I didn't need the input of someone who was just introduced to the situation. Only you really know yourself as a sexual being. We, as human beings, desire a partner who is understanding and accepting of us. It makes us feel comfortable when we are with a person who knows us. This happens best over time, when trust can be established. For someone you are newly dating to come in and try to tell you how wrong your ways are and how different they are from you only drives the two of you further apart. For me, the more distance between me and the person I am with, the less I think we should be together. I end up wanting to say, "You're right, we are different. In fact, what are we even doing together? I need to find someone I am more compatible with!"

At some point in their lives, nearly everyone has looked for a mate. Even the die-hard single guys in their forties who declare they only want to have sex with young women and will be bachelors forever break down once in a while. My friend Thomas is an aging British rock star who is still living the rock 'n' roll lifestyle. I often saw him alone at parties and other events in which everyone else had a date. He stayed strong and defiantly single till the day we were having lunch and over a pizza he asked me "Do you know any young birds you could set me up with?" I told him that I knew a lot of pretty girls but none of them would be into just having sex with him and not expecting more. He said quietly, "Well that's okay, I don't mind if they want to hang around a bit longer. I could do that."

Some women seek relationships as cures for their screwed-up lives. For instance, I often hear, "My job sucks; I hate my life, I'm broke but if I just had a boyfriend everything would be okay." Some women look for relationships to save them, both financially and emotionally, and many times it happens. The only problem is that when the relationship is over, or there is trouble with it, the woman is destroyed. She has nothing to fall back on. It is so important to love yourself and get a life of your own before adding someone else to the mix.

Katie Moran

I know many women who search frantically for the perfect man online. One girl I know will not let an hour pass without checking her Friendster.com, Match.com, and MySpace.com accounts. I know other people who have carried on entire relationships online. Maybe it's a good idea—some research shows Internet relationships that turn into real, "physical," relationships are more successful than conventional ones. My brother Nick met this girl online and spent months talking to her back and forth. They wrote each other every single day and he looked forward to her e-mails and new photos. By the time they met they knew everything about each other, which is great.

As an artist, I like to get to know people through writing first because it shows me how they express themselves and if they have the ability to put their feelings into words. However, you have to take into consideration the possibility that your Internet date may be less than honest. My brother eventually found out that this girl had painted an untruthful picture of herself online. Although she was intelligent and sweet she lied about her age, posting pictures that were easily a decade old. By the time Nick finally went on a date with her, he found himself out with the same girl he had grown to care about via e-mail, only now she was insecure because she had been dishonest about her age and weight problem. The difference was so drastic that he felt betrayed. He said if she had been honest from the get-go he would have been fine with it, as he is attracted to bigger women.

I don't know anyone who is attracted to insecurity and dishonesty, so to avoid getting hurt by online dating be honest about who you are from the beginning. Even if some people pass you by, the person you are meant to be with will be attracted to the real you. Remember, a relationship rarely works when it begins under false pretenses.

A friend of mine named Karen was convinced that this guy Jude was the right guy for her. She wanted to marry him the first time she met him. Just like me with my lover Laura, Karen had fallen into "insta-love." Karen was insta in love with Jude but he was the head of a self-help-type empire. She was a Christian but she decided to convert to his fly-by-night religion and spent thousands of dollars on workbooks, classes, and retreat weekends to find herself. She did find herself; she found herself out of a man. All of her friends were relieved, including me; she had reduced herself to something akin to a cult member in order to try to fit into this guy's lifestyle. Meanwhile, Jude did not practice what he preached. She caught him in bed with a hooker who had a knife in one hand and a whip in the other. He was all tied up and bound, looking like a victim of the Inquisition.

I have interviewed many men and women about the search for a mate and I hear the same answers over and over again. The most common reason people go out looking for a new lover, boyfriend, girlfriend, or fling is because they have just broken up with someone and want to forget about it. After break-ups, the next step seems to be getting back on the dating bicycle and trying to find a new sex symbol to ride. My friend Renee made an interesting point. She said that after she broke up with her boyfriend Jeremy she felt that she had thrown away a lot of precious time and that her relationship had been a complete waste of two years of her life.

After the break-up, Renee immediately went out with her friends in search of someone better to take his place. She wanted to erase the mistake of being with him. In her mind, she had lost a part of herself and the only way to redeem this was to find someone to compensate for the loss. Her search for a new love was not only a "cure" for her broken heart, but also a coping mechanism for how badly she felt about her bad dating decisions with Jeremy.

The search for your "perfect" mate is like trying to fulfill some kind of ideal that does not really exist. After all, if I

Katie Moran

waited the rest of my life for my dream partner; a fabulously successful model who lived in a gigantic beach house, insisted on me never working a day in my life, adored me and allowed me to sleep with whomever I pleased, well, I'd be waiting through three lifetimes before that would occur. We are all human and we are all flawed. We have to meet the person who is flawed in ways we can accept and love, have a lot of laughs and fun with, and also be aroused by. That person is out there for each and every one of us. Some are lucky and meet several people who fill the criteria in one lifetime and date or marry two or three soul mates in a lifetime. My close friends are like a group of soul mates and I didn't go out scouring the city and searching for them. We found each other, somehow, and it was destiny.

My friend Talia was a search-a-holic constantly on the look-out for the man of her dreams. She joined every online personals site there was. She even went to those dating lunches where you meet a handful of single men in one meal. She was a girl on a mission. Yet, like every other woman I interviewed for this book, Talia had to admit that when you go and look for love it never works out.

Talia's dating record was fatal. She was on a serious losing streak and it became painful to watch her repeat behaviors over and over again. All of the men she met were through the Internet personals such as Matchmaker and Match.com. She would meet a man, they would go out on a casual date, talk on the phone, and get to know each other. They would go on a second date, talk on the phone, e-mail each other; Talia would find something to get jealous about, go psycho, the guy would leave, and Talia would become even more pathetic. All of Talia's friends would tell her, "You have to take it easy on these guys. Don't push them so hard . . . it is obvious that they like you but you are forcing the issue!" She wouldn't heed our warning.

I remember this one poor chap named Carl. He was the

sweetest guy and when Talia introduced me to him I could tell that he liked her. I thought to myself that there was no way she could screw this one up because he was so crazy about her. Well, I was wrong. She felt that Carl was "the one" and made the mistake of telling him how important he was to her after only their second date. She called him incessantly, even disrupting his out-of-town business meeting and conference calls to whine to him on the phone about how much she missed him. She forwarded me an e-mail she sent him raking him over the coals for not calling her enough while he was in Scottsdale. This was after their third date. I think I actually pulled the covers over my head in horror as I read her words to him on my laptop screen. It was painful to see how she had destroyed this new relationship.

Talia's problem was that she lacked fulfillment in her own emotional life and expected too much from and relied too heavily on virtual strangers (Carl, in this case) to give her everything she needed and lacked in her own emotional life. She so badly wanted him to fill all the voids she had within her that she committed the ultimate crime; the unforgivable turn-off for a man . . . she was the proverbial needy woman. Talia has scared off so many men I have lost count. Sadly, she is still scaring them off today. In fact, she even ran out of men to scare off and is now dating women and scaring them off too!

I enjoy being single, but I admit that when it gets boring, I have activated the search button. It never works. The one thing I have learned on my many escapades is this: Stop looking for the perfect mate. The best time to meet someone is when you are not searching. I think men can smell desperation. I think you can meet someone great in those brief moments when you are just being yourself.

I was taken off guard one early Sunday morning in Hollywood. It was really late, around 3 AM, and I was tired after a long night of working on a story. I was also hungry. I got in the

Katie Moran

car, dog in the backseat, and went down the street to the only place that was open, a taco shop. There were the usual Hollywood types there, people half cocked from partying and going crazy with the munchies. I didn't fit in wearing my pajamas, boxer briefs and a worn out T-shirt. My hair was in a rubber band and I had no make-up on. Everyone else was dressed up, the girls in tight little outfits and guys in their best pants and shined shoes. I ducked into a corner to scarf down two chicken tacos without being noticed. There was a shortage of chairs in the joint so this really cute guy asked if he could sit at my table. I reluctantly said "okay" and he smiled and sat down, introducing himself as Rob.

He tried to strike up a conversation and within a couple of minutes I realized he was trying to pick me up! I flat out asked him why he was interested in me since I looked like I just rolled out of bed. He said that he could tell that there was a nice body under the T-shirt and long hair under the mess, which he liked. I was surprised at his approach but I took his number anyway and called him the next day. We went out but, even though he was a real sweetheart, I was not really attracted to him. I still love the way we met; it was so impromptu and natural.

When I ended my own personal search for a boyfriend a few years back and allowed a friend to set me up on a blind date, love found its way to me quite unexpectedly. After long and treacherous nights filled with boring conversation and dates with about as much sex appeal as a pasty Euro-trash guy with bitch tits and BO playing with himself in public, I finally let my friend Mariah set me up with a coworker of hers, Danny Fast.

I hate blind dates. It is the fear of disappointment that keeps me from going on too many of them. Why are blind dates so awful? Well, it is at least partly the fear of the unknown. There is also something off putting about the way blind dates mess up the best part of conventional dating; that amazing feeling of meeting someone on your own, that natural attraction that brings two people together. That feeling just gets nixed on blind dates. I have found myself sitting across from a specimen about as interesting as a doorknob, and probably about as tall as one too, thinking to myself, "How in the hell did I get into this and how long do I have to wait before it is rude to run out of this restaurant screaming?"

Danny was different. I had talked to him several times on the phone and was instantly at ease with his cute laugh and familiar banter. Also, his thick New Jersey accent conjured up visualizations of making out in the backseat of classic Pontiacs and souped-up Camaros. Although I am from the West Coast and had never participated in that "Jersey" style of lovin', I have a vivid imagination, and the thought of something so lurid and tacky aroused me. I was dreaming of him before I even met him.

Danny showed up a few minutes late with a smile and a bottle of wine still in the paper bag. He was so cute. He wore baggy jeans and a striped polo shirt. He had brown hair and a slightly crooked nose from playing hockey. He looked like the East Coast version of Colin Farrell. Perfect. Like the experienced dater I am, I took him to one of my favorite bars, the Good Luck Bar. True to its name, I have always found good luck at the Good Luck Bar—it's probably the effects of the potent drinks mixed by the seasoned bartender that do it. I love the Good Luck Bar; no matter how bad the day or the date, I can go there and meet someone else or find an old friend to make the night better. It's dark, out of the way, and sexy.

Danny was good luck from the start. My friend was right; he was a really down-to-earth, great guy. He sent money to his mom every month to help her out and was putting himself through school. He was authentic East Coast charm with nothing fake or pretentious about him and that is hard to find in Los Angeles. We opened up to each other right away. He was a great storyteller and he took me back to the times he was a

Katie Moran

little kid causing trouble on the streets he grew up on. But my luck with Danny extended far beyond the mental connection and stories we shared that night. It also continued on past the strong drinks and into the passionate sex we shared in the spa that night. The spa, the grass next to the spa, and, of course, the bed of the house where I was living at the time.

Who knew that a reluctant blind date would turn out to be my boyfriend of almost a year? It was an unexpected gift and something I was not searching for. The next day he called me at 10 AM to tell me what a great time he had. He told everyone in the office, including my best friend, that it was the best date he ever had, an eleven out of ten. Of course, by the end of the day everyone assumed we had sex the night before but I didn't care. I knew he and I would be together again and again . . . and again. He was so sweet and caring. Every day Danny would call me twice a day at work, once at 10 AM and again at 5 PM to see what I would be doing that night. Eventually my crazy lifestyle took its toll; I was too psychotic and unsettled in my own life to appreciate what a good thing I had with Danny. I was still partying with my friends too much and working insane hours at a job I hated; I had little room left in my life for this relationship. What a mistake! He was good-looking, motivated, thoughtful, and sweet. Not to mention, the sex was amazing.

Austin still held the record as the best lover I had ever experienced but Danny now carried a close second. Everywhere we went he looked out for me. I was quite the drunk during my days with him so he would buy me an extra bottle of vodka to keep in my purse when we went out to bars. He played street hockey every Sunday in Venice Beach and one day he even spent the afternoon trying to teach me how to play. He enrolled me on a beginner's team and after ten minutes I was exhausted and realized it was far more pleasurable to sit on the sidelines and admire the hot sweaty guys rolling back and forth in the sun. Some of the sexiest guys on the planet play hockey. If you have access to a beach or rink where guys play hockey for fun, check it out! They are much sexier than the polo players (who turn out to be a disappointment in bed from what I have heard).

I still regret screwing up my relationship with Danny, taking him for granted, and acting like an asshole in the months that followed our break-up. I guess I just wasn't ready for the real thing. He went away for some summer college exchange program and I held it against him even though he called me every other day. While he was gone I did my fair share of sleeping around, with both guys and girls. Kristina was still loosely in the picture which only made things crazier. The early twenties are a fanatical time for a lot of people but they seemed to be magnified for me. I heard Kim Catrall's character on *Sex and the City* say, "I am a try-sexual; I'll try anything once." I took her philosophy to heart.

I wanted to experience it all and my desires became a selfish addiction in the end. Danny was a casualty of my fun-loving ways. I really liked him but it was not going to the love stage. When he came home, I was rude to him because he had given himself an at-home haircut that made him look like a prisoner on death row. I made the mistake of telling him that, instead of welcoming him back with a big hug and a kiss. He realized right then that I was a bitch and someone he didn't want to continue a relationship with. His smile melted away and I saw his heart shatter right in front of me as I stood there rudely, not wanting to touch him.

In retrospect I realize that I didn't feel I deserved that kind of respect and loyalty from another human being. I was used to disposable relationships and guys who would move across country to escape me. I was not used to someone who wanted to stick around and stick it out. I kick myself now. He was the kind of guy who would come over to my house at any hour of the night to bring me ginger ale and crackers and massage my

Katie Moran

feet when I was sick. Danny didn't have a bad bone in his body. My best friend still gives me grief for screwing that one up. Sometimes friends know better who is suited for you than you know yourself. Dating a guy like Danny—pure, good hearted, honest, and loving—was truly a stroke of good luck.

6

The Ex Files

Break-ups are not easy. Even a mutual split is tough because there are so many feelings involved. And if you are like me, change, even for the better, is a major emotional adjustment. There are many types of break-ups and exes; some relationships end slowly and gradually, while others end overnight. My friend Dina loved her boyfriend Sean. They were engaged to be married; yet they fought constantly. Dina tried to explain it to me by saying, "I love him but I don't love us." They broke up, spent some time apart, cried, and did the "bonus" sex thing . . . who hasn't slept with an ex at least once? Sometimes it is even better than commitment sex. No relationship, no hang-ups, just fun.

And now, several years later, her ex-boyfriend is married with a baby and she is still friends with him. They occasionally have lunch together and when Sean and his wife want an evening out Dina even babysits for them. A round of applause for Dina's high level of maturity—I'm not completely there yet. Then there is the other kind of ex, the one who is still in love with you, probably the one that you dumped. He or she never quite got over you and wants to maintain a friendship.

There is a line in the song "Ex-Girlfriend" by No Doubt that goes, "I kind of always knew I'd end up your ex-girlfriend." Every time I hear this song I smile because I have had this same feeling too many times myself. At the beginning of some relationships it feels as if it is too good to be true. The kind of relationship where you are way too much in love way too fast and everything feels so good and so right that you think to yourself "This is it, this is right. This must be whom I am meant to be with. It is fate . . . right?" Then you find out who they really are and it all crumbles. But, right before everything falls apart, at least for me, there is this moment where I think to myself, "I don't think this is going to work. It's too perfect." Then there have been other times, like with Austin, when even though I was in it for the fun and would have liked the good times to last forever, I always knew he would wind up my ex-boyfriend sooner or later. Important aspects of a partnership, such as communication, were lacking between us and promised to bring an inevitable end to our relationship.

My friend Lisa was thirty-two when she met this great guy, Dan. I told her that I was sure they were going to get married. She said, "Oh, I am not so sure about that. I have no idea where this is going." The look on her face showed me that she did not care either way and that it was not something she had given much thought. The beauty of that relationship was that, from the start, Lisa had no expectations of Dan. She never once speculated where things were going nor did she worry about marriage or moving in, the types of things that some women stress about, causing unnecessary damage to a relationship.

Lisa never did move in with Dan before they got married. She lived at her parents' house for more than four years while they dated. Then, on a fun weekend getaway in the mountains, Dan surprised her by popping the question. He had the perfect ring picked; Lisa was in shock. When she got home she called me and told me that she had no idea whatsoever that he was even thinking about marriage. She was too busy having a good time with him and just letting things progress naturally. Some men need a little nudge now and then, I hear, but Dan was a person who let things happen when they were supposed to. He said his favorite thing about Lisa was that she never pressured him, making him fall in love with her even more. They both had confidence that things would work out the way they were meant to.

They are married now and have two great children. They treat each other with kindness, generosity, and respect every day. I wish everyone had the gift of leaving things alone. I have a few exes who have the title of "ex" because they were too concerned with where the relationship was going. They became obsessed with controlling my feelings and decisions, pushing me away even more.

At this point in my life I have no desire to get married. Not because I have not met the "right" person, but because there is nothing appealing about marriage to me. Being with one person for the rest of my life sounds like a bad dream. My friend Mariah, who just recently married her boyfriend of seven years, feels differently about it. She is one of those girls, and sometimes I feel like I am the only exception, that always wanted a husband and always dreamed of being with one person her entire life.

That prospect of marriage excited Mariah, it felt right to her, she wanted it. It wasn't that she was daydreaming about the white dress and the big wedding, although she had both of those; she wanted the life partner and the family. She did not want another ex-boyfriend. I remember when they would have

Katie Moran

problems, problems like cheating or addiction that would have been fatal to one of my relationships, they would never run. They would stick around and work them out. It was impressive for someone like me, who either runs from a bad situation or is run from at full speed. I know Mariah will stay with this guy till death do they part. Ex-husband is not even in her vocabulary.

My Aunt Priscilla, who wears big sunglasses with a giant rhinestone "P" in the corner of the lens and drives a gold Cadillac, has so many ex-husbands that it is getting difficult to remember what name goes with what face. She brings one along to family functions sometimes, dragging them around like a big purse. I asked her why she has so many ex-husbands and she replied, "Hormones."

She married her first husband when she was very young. He was a mobster named Frankie and he pulled one of the biggest bank robberies of all time while they were married. She was put on the stand by the FBI and even made the front page of the *New York Times*. When Frankie was arrested and sent away on unrelated charges, Priscilla fled to the West Coast, later filing for divorce. While working as a go-go dancer on Sunset Strip, she met another man, a club owner named Harold. She stayed married to him throughout her thirties. She tired of him and moved on to a golf pro and then a restaurant owner. I never met her fifth husband because the marriage was so short. She said she never had sex outside of marriage, which I am not so sure I believe. But she claims her fidelity was the reason she would grow so tired of having sex with the same man and developed the itch to be with someone new. She never had children to keep her tied to one guy.

After menopause, she began taking estrogen supplements. Now, at age seventy-something (she would kill me if I revealed her real age), she looks about fifty-eight and has a big bright smile and the breasts of a thirty-year-old. Last Christmas she was dancing around the living room, grabbing my cousins' hands and spinning them around. I was tired from eating too much and felt about ninety, slumped into the couch while she just kept on dancing. I thought she might OD on estrogen, she looked so pumped full of hormones. Yet I would rather feel as good as her than as bad as I feel at times, some fifty years younger. Everyone was admiring her dancing, and she yelled out, "Grab my ass! Come on, grab it! Feel how tight my ass is!" Since I was sitting on the couch at ass level, I gave it a squeeze. It was tighter than a twenty-year-old guy's butt! It was very impressive for a lady so old most of her friends were consumed with playing bridge and doing crossword puzzles. Instead, there she was, dancing wildly around the room.

Due to Priscilla's increasingly excessive make-up use, I recently gave her a new nickname, Aunt Face. One Saturday I called up Aunt Face for a favor; when she finally answered the phone she was groggy at two o'clock in the afternoon. I asked her if I could come over because I wanted to use her fax machine. She told me that James was over and they were sleeping in because they had a long night drinking and doing other stuff. I cringed at the "other stuff" remark. I assumed that her "no sex without marriage" rule had been abandoned. James was her thirty-nine-year-old boyfriend. Yes, no need to go back and re-read that. James is thirty-nine and Aunt Face is seventy-something. Of course, James thinks that she is in her fifties and has no idea that he is sleeping with someone nearly forty years older than he is! I wonder if he ever found out that little fact if he would make her his ex-girlfriend. I hope that she never has to find that out. That is, unless she wants to move on and is ready for a newer, younger model! Priscilla is surely talented at making ex-husbands.

The sight or thought of an ex can be severely painful, even months after the break-up. Poor Bobby is a perfect example of the tortured-by-the-ex syndrome. Bobby thought he had met the love of his life in Jason. They both loved Reese Witherspoon

Katie Moran

films, shopping for Diesel clothes, SUVs, the beach, and each other's attention. One night Bobby and Jason took Mia and me out to dinner. Mia and I were in the back seat of the car and they were in the front. I remember, they were sitting so close together I thought Bobby would fall over into Jason's lap and lose control of the car. The things they said to each other were sickeningly sweet like, "Did you get the note I left for you this morning next to your waffles with maple syrup that isn't nearly as dreamy and tasty as your kisses?" Ugh, I wanted to gag. It was so irritating to be around them.

Bobby turned into an entirely different person. He ignored all his girl friends because he was too busy picking up Jason's dry cleaning and walking Jason's dog. I missed Bobby but at the same time I was happy for him because I knew he had found what he was looking for, the boyfriend. Jason left Bobby after five weeks, writing him one of those "sweetie" notes while Bobby was sleeping and then walking out the door for good. Bobby woke up to find the break-up letter, but this time there was no breakfast and syrup to accompany it. Jason said things were moving too fast and that he was overwhelmed. This translates to, "You were smothering me." Now Bobby was back in our lives full force, ordering pizza after pizza from my couch and watching *Queer Eye for the Straight Guy* and every home-decorating channel possible screaming at the screen, "I deserve a house and a husband, you fucking bitch!"

I finally realized how badly hurt Bobby was by Jason's departure when he ran into him at my house party. I don't know why I continue to have house parties; this year, on my birthday I had 200 people at my house and it was a total disaster. It was the most out-of-control party I have ever thrown, even the legendary party that I threw at my parents' house when I was in college couldn't compare. . . . They were living on the East Coast at the time and left the house in the care of my high-school-aged brother. He and I threw a party that went on for three weeks straight. People were drinking cheap liquor, getting the dog stoned (I was not happy about that), having sex in the bathrooms, and throwing things in the pool. The party ended when I fell very ill. I developed pneumonia and could not get out of bed because I was so exhausted. I had to call my grandmother to come and kick everyone out; one would think I'd have learned my lesson about house parties.

Though still a total disaster, my birthday party was at least a more grown-up disaster. By this I mean that the cheap booze had been replaced by expensive vodka and whiskey, the weed was now accompanied by ecstasy and cocaine, and the police came instead of my grandma. Bobby was still distraught from the break-up when he showed up at the party wearing a hideous vintage faux fur coat he had plucked out of a garage sale earlier that day. Before I could warn him, Bobby spotted Jason by the food table. I felt horribly responsible for Jason's presence at the party, but I had said everyone could come and Jason was a friend of a friend and well, you know the drill. I would have had a hard time telling him that he was not invited when 200 other people were.

Bobby looked like someone who had just been caught by the *COPS* camera crew. His expression alternated between pissed off and scared and he clearly couldn't decide whether to make a run for it or just lay down on the floor and cry. Instead he decided to lambaste me and then run to his car. I think he waited until he was safely in his car before he let go and cried all the way home. He wouldn't speak to me or our other friends for weeks after that incident. Even though their relationship had been over for four months, Bobby's heart broke all over again every time he saw Jason and it was just as painful as the first time he read that break-up note.

Unfortunately for Bobby, Jason-the-ex was still haunting him a year later. Bobby had been living in this great rent-controlled apartment in West Hollywood for years, paying $650 a month

Katie Moran

89

for a place his neighbors were paying $1,300 for. Finding a nice place in West Hollywood is tough and most apartments have several applicants. Jason just so happened to apply for one such apartment right below Bobby. Even with intense pleading and flirting, Bobby could not sway the manager to decline Jason's application and he moved in right underneath Bobby. Now to Jason, this was no big deal. He barely even remembered their blink-of-an-eye relationship but a year later Bobby was still reeling from the break-up. Bobby got his chance at revenge though; he lived above Jason for a month, banging his feet on the floor and playing Bette Davis movies on the highest volume his surround sound could manage. He would scream out the window, "I am on top now, loser!" This time, Bobby won the ex game. Jason moved out. No one bothered to tell Bobby that Jason had moved in with his brand new boyfriend. We just let him bask in his success for once.

Many different things can happen with exes. Some exes become fuck buddies . . . some become great fuck buddies. I dated one guy for a short period of time before we both grew bored of each other. I was about to graduate college and was feeling very full of myself with my newly acquired education. This guy was definitely a not-going-anywhere-anytime-soon kind of guy. He liked to hang out at my house because he did not even have his own room. He rented someone's couch. Yes, couch rental is an actual form of dwelling for some people. He was too lazy to even think of something to say. When I remember him, I can only picture him lying down, on my couch. Or, lying down on his couch when I would make the trip out there to the marina to spend some time in the filth of his apartment shared with four other twenty-something guys.

The relationship did not last long but one night, after we had broken up, I had come back from a club after drinking and called him. He came over, on his scooter, and we had sex. It was fun and in the morning, he left. We used each other for sex frequently, and there was never any problem—no drama and no expectations. One time he even brought me an In'n'Out cheeseburger and a shake. I thought that was a really nice gesture; but then that is what happens when you live without any expectations—a burger makes you happy.

Having someone in your life that you are comfortable enough with to continue a sexual relationship is great. It is probably safer than sleeping with multiple partners and more rewarding. Both you and your "buddy" know each other's likes and dislikes in bed and can communicate on a trusting level. A sexual relationship is like any other relationship; it takes work and time to develop something functional and enjoyable. But when you meet someone special and it can lead to a potential relationship, drop the fuck buddy. I know a girl who used to make a habit of letting two guys occupy one space and it never worked out for her. The "buddy" was always waiting in the wings but the prospective boyfriend could inevitably sense another dog roaming the block and headed out to find his own territory.

Some exes become friends, neighbors, or distant memories, but the worst is when exes become stalkers. I know this is a serious subject for many women and men. In my case, these "stalkers" turned out to be relatively harmless if not just completely annoying. But for some people, stalking can turn frightening and sometimes deadly, so always look at a stalking situation with seriousness.

When I first started writing, I sat at a desk that anyone could walk right up to and see me on my computer typing away. The office where I worked was right at the beach near a popular boardwalk so I was used to people wandering in and out and asking me for directions. One morning I was lost in thought when I felt someone looking at me. It was a breezy summer day and I thought the person staring at me was another lost tourist on his way to the Ferris wheel. It wasn't. It was this guy I had

Katie Moran

gone out with a couple of times and now there he was, looking down at me, blank eyed and expressionless. I didn't know how long he had been there but I found out later from some other co-workers that he had been by every day that week looking for me. The worst part was that I had never told him where I worked but somehow he found out.

Other times, I would be watching TV and see headlights shine through the front window of my living room. I would look up to see his blue Camry turn around in the cul-de-sac. I felt sick to my stomach that this guy had taken away my sense of privacy. It was irritating but, luckily, he eventually stopped. I am guilty of some mild stalking myself. When I stop dating someone that I really liked, I do a drive-by. I slowly drive by their house to see if they are home, who is over, and to try to catch a glimpse of them. I don't know what I would do if I was ever caught in the act. I must have gone past Laura's friend's place three or four times to see if she was still in town. One time I caught another guy, an ex of mine, doing a drive-by of my place and I invited him in and we had sex. He was a nice guy, good-looking and honest. I knew that it would make him happy and Oprah was a re-run so it seemed like a good idea. It reinforced the behavior, however, and he was back the next week. This time I wasn't outside to greet him.

The most pathetic aspect of stalking is when a female ex becomes a stalker. I was doing an interview with a variety of women on the topic of bisexuality and one girl admitted to me that she had never kissed a woman. After several meetings with her, it became apparent that she wanted her first kiss to be with me. I was flattered, of course, and finally yielded to her advances. We kissed and it was awful. Her energy was aggressive and her kissing style grotesque. It was one of the worst kisses I have ever had.

Of course, for her it was a monumental moment because she was kissing a girl for the first time. I was flattered, but I really didn't want to be some girl's training wheels, and I felt I had learned my lesson from this one kiss. She did drive-bys of my house for weeks. My roommate would see her and say, "Oh there goes that maroon car again." One time around 3 AM, I was sitting on my bedroom floor typing on my laptop. My dog looked up toward the window and a split second later I did to. I saw her face framed in the window, clear as day in the moonlight. She ducked down but being nearly six feet tall, she couldn't hide too well. I was freaked out to say the least. I ran to the front of my house and looked out the window to see the little maroon car speed away. Another time, about a week later, she rang the doorbell at around the same time, 3 AM. I opened the door, pissed off, and yelled at her for her rudeness.

Believe it or not, we became friends about six months after that. She met someone new and was way over me. I was in a dating rut and she turned out to be a fun person to hang out with. Of course, six months more and true to form, she became a psycho again. This time it manifested itself in a different way. She accused me of saying something to someone about something or other, some bullshit. I do not do the he-said-she-said game so our friendship ended there. Luckily she does not have my new address.

If I have trouble with stalkers I can only imagine how bad it must be for celebrities. It is like they have millions of ex-boyfriends and ex-girlfriends watching their every move, passively or more directly stalking them. Recently, I heard someone say right in front of one particular thirty-something, prime-time TV star, "Oh there goes so and so, you know she had *more* plastic surgery. Damn, she's ugly in person. (pause) Oooh, where she goin'? Let's go have lunch there and try to get a table next to her." It reminds me of having an ex who still wants to be with you and wants to know your every move to make sure you aren't doing anything fabulous without them. But, when they

Katie Moran

do know what is happening in your life, they grow judgmental, bitter, and angry.

Then there are the exes who become phone stalkers. I am sure everyone can relate to the phone stalker. I went out with this guy one time and then told him I felt that we should just be friends. Who was I fooling? We made plans to go surfing at eight o'clock in the morning. Now, all of my friends know that as much as I would like to get up on a Saturday morning and go surfing, it is never going to happen. I am much more of the sunset surf type of gal. Anyway, I told him the night before, "If I don't answer the phone, just go without me. I have a tendency to sleep in."

True to form, I slept in. He kept calling and calling and calling me. My phone was in the other room and I could hear its constant yet faint ringing. Luckily I am a heavy sleeper and was able to tune it out. He called me from 7 AM until 1 PM. When I finally did get up, I checked my caller ID and he had filled the entire list. He had called at least fifty times.

That night I e-mailed him and told him that I was sorry about not waking up, but I had warned him. He asked me if I wanted to order in Chinese the next night and I wrote him back a firm, "No." I was thinking to myself "Isn't ordering in something reserved for good friends and lovers?" He called me for weeks, never leaving a message. He called me from vacation, he called me from work, and he called me from his mom's house. He never once tried blocking his number. At least he wasn't being sneaky. I finally had to change my number because besides this guy I had another ex, from about a year before that, who had started calling and wanting me to explain why I didn't want to be with him and what the other guys I was dating had that he didn't. No answer was ever good enough and he resorted to phone stalking. He would call twenty or thirty times in a row before finally giving up until later on that day. I called up the phone company, changed my number, and peace was restored.

As painful as it is, try not to pick up the phone after a break-up. Leave the relationship with some dignity. There have been times when I dial an ex's phone number but I'm usually quick enough to hang up before it can even ring once. I stare at the person's number in my mobile phone wondering if I should delete it or not. Every time I go against my instinct and give in to the desire to call, I end up either getting back together with the person and regretting it or having sex with them and sometimes regretting it. In worst-case scenarios these phone calls reveal that your ex is dating other people and totally over you or talking to each other is just awkward and reminds you that you're no longer together.

My friend Kayla had a boyfriend whom she liked as a person but who could not maintain a hard-on. Eventually the endless nights of sexual frustration were too much for her and she broke up with him; he gave her "blue clit," my friend Talia's term for the female equivalent of blue balls. Kayla thought nothing more of it until a year after the break-up, when her ex asked to take her to lunch. It became obvious halfway through the lunch that he had been taking Viagra and wanted to prove himself to her one last time, going so far as to press himself against her so she could feel his raging hard-on. When Kayla emphatically refused his offer, he began calling her five times a day and stalking her. Kayla changed her number and moved. Who can blame her? There is nothing worse than a loser with an artificial hard-on who wants to use it. Her ex had turned from a decent person into a guy who acted like an old dog with a bad itch that rubs up against poles, walls, and any leg it can find. Kayla was not in the mood to be some ex's scratching post.

I am not really friends with any of my male exes. The females, on the other hand, are more difficult to part with. The

Katie Moran

girls are friends and in some cases, I become closer to them after we stop sleeping together because we share the special bond of having an often secret sexual past together. Guys will be guys, fairly predictable and steadfast in their ways, but girls seem more likely to change and grow. I have seen some of the immature girls from my past metamorphose into strong women. As for the guys, I talk to some of them on occasion and we have made peace with the past. Some I miss, and for some I am glad that they have moved on and are happy. I wished them well and we went our separate ways . . . except for one.

One of the most mortifying pieces of information I have heard was that my ex Austin got hitched. I am not a malicious person, but I would have preferred finding Austin's carcass on the highway picked clean by vultures than hearing that he had gotten married to a twenty-three-year-old Swede and that they were moving back to Sweden. For me, Austin was that "open door" ex, you know, the one you always hoped you would get back together with. So hearing that the door was closed for good made me reflect on my own life. Am I emotionally un-available? Yeah, but so is he. Why did he marry her but break up with me so callously? The fact that he was able to commit to another woman hurt my feelings.

I called Austin one day out of the blue to see what he was doing. I thought if he wasn't around, I could at least catch up with his parents, who were always nice to me. The last time I saw Austin we were both at a birthday party. As we talked I could feel the old, familiar chemistry, and I could tell that he knew there was still something there as well. Everything was going great until he saw some drunk guy hanging on me as if he knew me. I recognized the look in Austin's eyes that told me a red flag had been thrown up. I could tell he believed I was the same wild and crazy party girl that would only leave him feel-ing empty and alone. I wasn't. Seeing him at the party had made me realize how ready I was to be with him. I knew that there was no one I would rather be with and that this time the attraction had gone further than just sex. We left the party that night and went our separate ways. The phone call was my last attempt to make a connection.

Austin was shocked to hear my voice and I could hear a lump in his throat; he sounded as if he was a doctor giving a prognosis to the family of a dying patient. He said, "Wow, I can't believe you are calling me now. You have really interesting timing. I wish you had called a few weeks ago. I just got married." And I said the first thing that came out of my mouth, something really truthful and real, "Why?" He said, "It was just something I wanted to do." So, I said the only thing I could think of, "Congratulations." Of course, what I really meant was, "I hope you get a divorce and call me." We talked for a while but it was strained. I told him I would e-mail him in Sweden and he actually said, "No, don't. It's not a good idea." Now I was on the opposite side of the ex fence and it wasn't fun. I was being ex-ed out.

I think everyone has that one person in their past that was truly special. And when you are alone and sick of being single, you can dream of one day being back with him or her and everything is okay. All that "what is meant to be will be" and "something better is planned for you" did not help me much the day I found out about Austin. I ended up going to my best friend's house. She was of no help. All of her exes are still in love with her. She can go back to any of her "open doors" at any time. So I called my new flame. No answer.

I went home, ate some chocolate pudding, played with the dog, and finally called Kristina, who confirmed that the new wife was plainer than bargain-brand yogurt. I lay back on the bed with a smile on my face—this information helped a great deal. I dug for details and she said not to worry, the chick was ugly and I was cute and all those other nice things friends say to make you feel better. Hey, it may be petty, but it made me

Katie Moran

feel a little better that day. It took me a while to come to terms with the past, but I was finally able to close the door on that relationship with Austin. It really was over—the ex file had closed on him. I still haven't had an orgasm that quite compared to the ones I had with Austin, but now I have a standard to measure them by, and relationships that are filled with far more communication, laughter, and meaning.

7

Chemistry . . . or Chemical Imbalance?

Chemistry at work between two people is a cool thing. Imagine seeing someone sitting at a table in a crowded outdoor restaurant, the sun shining on their blond, brown, black, bald, whatever does it for you, head. You catch their eye. A coy smile comes over your face and you blush. He or she approaches. It is magic. The air between you is thick and amorous, the conversation is amazing, and the sexual attraction is so strong it feels as if this person already has his hands all over you.

Flip side: You meet someone in a bar, they are cute and funny but it is loud and your friends want to leave. You quickly exchange numbers and agree to a dinner date. Whether there is chemistry or not will have to be revealed later. Meeting someone with whom you find that connection, the physical and mental spark known as chemistry, is rare. I never know who is going to turn me on.

So we all know what it feels like when there is chemistry. It feels good. It feels right. All of the senses, the body and the mind, are standing at attention, excited and on. But what if there is no chemistry . . . when are you sure of that? I often mistake a high-energy freak or an intoxicated young thing as my soul mate instead of just my drug of choice for an evening of fun.

My friend Sheryl's dry spell had finally ended. She was so thrilled to have found some cock that she was regularly skipping out on her job as a hospital psychologist to go and have sex. Sheryl was heavily into this guy she was dating and he really did it for her . . . until he opened his mouth. He was completely out of his mind; crazy, irrational, and unreliable, but when they were in bed he took her on the ride of her life. She said the physical and sexual chemistry was incredible but mentally, well, she might as well have been talking to one of her patients. They just could not connect on an emotional level. She eventually burned out on the just-sex bit and had to let him go.

Luckily for Sheryl she met the man of her dreams shortly after. Actually, I met the man of her dreams and kismet took over. We were sitting at an outdoor coffee-house on Sunset Boulevard one afternoon with a group of friends. Two cute guys walked up and joined the group. Sheryl and I immediately perked up and shook their hands, purring out enthusiastic "Hi-iiis." You know the kind of "Hi" I am talking about. Not a simple, friendly "Hi, nice to meet you," but a long, slow "Hiiii" complete with eye contact and a seductive little smile. Brandon sat down next to me. He was sweet and friendly with that kind of cute young Jeremy Piven look that screamed, "I am not fat and bald yet, but as you can see by my hairline, I will be." The other guy was Jared. He was tall and handsome and though he did not say much I thought he was very attractive and had an air of success. When Sheryl asked if I was interested in Brandon I said, "He's cute but Jared is really the catch." At the time she did not agree.

We exchanged numbers with the new guys and a few days later Jared called Sheryl to ask her to babysit his puppy while he went away for the weekend. I could tell after a few meetings that he was interested in her because he was always making an excuse to see her. Jared was about ten years older than I was, much closer to Sheryl's age than mine, and they were both great-looking and Jewish; it was a match made in heaven, or at least temple. Sheryl asked me if it was okay if they went out on a date because she knew I thought he was hot. I told her to go for it. I had known all along that Jared was perfect, but for Sheryl, not myself. Sometimes friends know these things before we realize them for ourselves.

Sheryl and Jared went out on their first date and as soon as we spoke she had nothing but great things to report. She was so insanely attracted to him that she spent the whole first date fighting the urge drag him home and fuck him. Instead she went home and pulled out her old friend, the vibrator, to satiate her desires. The chemistry between Sheryl and Jared was so strong it was almost tangible. When they finally did start having sex, Sheryl reported to all of us that she was having it three or four times a day; they could not get enough of each other. From the start it was obvious Jared was the guy she would marry. Everything about their relationship was in synch, from the kind of cars they liked to the types of medication they took for their panic attacks.

And then there was me. Because one of my best friends was dating a guy whose best friend liked me, I was coerced into going out with the friend against my better judgment. Call it peer pressure or call it rationalization—maybe I just thought it

Katie Moran

would be fun if two best guy friends dated two best girl friends. Either way I ended up going out with Jared's best friend Brandon. What he and I had can only be described as part-time chemistry, sometimes lukewarm, sometimes a little steamier. We dated for a few months and even though he was a terrific guy our chemistry was never that great. Brandon deserved a girl that was more into him and I was never completely "there" in my attraction towards him.

I should have ended things with Brandon a lot sooner but I have a hard time breaking up with people I like, even when it is not working sexually. Brandon and I were more like friends than boyfriend/girlfriend. He was such a nice guy I didn't want to hurt his feelings and tell him that I was growing less and less attracted to him by the minute.

There was one night in particular that really drove it all home for me. We enjoyed dinner together before we went back to my place and started fooling around in my bed. Brandon went down on me and wanted me to return the favor. To me, blowjobs are very intimate and I would rather have intercourse than put my mouth on someone I don't care about. But I also felt that it was unfair since he just spent ten minutes in between my thighs and did a good job of it too.

I hate girls that will let a guy perform oral sex on them but will not return the favor or vice versa. So many guys want blowjobs but turn their nose up on performing oral sex on a girl. If you meet a guy like that, run the other way. It is indicative of a lot of other selfish characteristics that will show up later. Brandon was not selfish and he enjoyed sex with me very much—I wish I could have felt the same way but the chemistry was not there. When I went down, reached into his pants, and took his dick into my mouth, he laid back and a smile of complete ecstasy came across his face. Then I did what every man in his position fears the most; I stopped. I apologized but I told him I just wasn't feeling it. What bad timing, shame on me.

Brandon was really upset and wanted to take a cab home but I insisted on giving him a ride. Even though he must have had the worst case of blue balls he had halfway forgiven me by the time I dropped him off across town. I see him around sometimes and we are cordial to each other. He gives me a generous hug, the kind with the lame pat on the back that says, "You still suck but I am bigger than that."

One phenomenon that took me a while to figure out is one-sided chemistry. Have you ever been so attracted to someone and felt intense electricity between you and another person only to find out that you were the only person that felt it? I was completely taken with a guy named David. When we stood close together I felt a magnet pulling our hearts, and our genitals, together. I was so attracted to him and thought that we were so good for each other that I could barely see straight. My eyes wouldn't focus when I was near him.

We were both young and although we occasionally fooled around together he told me that he did not want a relationship. I thought he was lying; there was no way he couldn't have felt the chemistry burning between us. Years later I saw David strolling down Santa Monica Boulevard in a white Dolce and Gabbana tank top and strategically ripped Armani Exchange jeans, hair highlighted, and gabbing away on his clear mobile phone. The boy was so gay! Usually I can spot a gay guy a mile away, even a guy who is in complete denial and still closeted, like David was. This was the only time I ever found myself turned on by a gay guy.

When one-sided chemistry happens in reverse, and somebody I have no interest in is convinced there are sparks between us, I feel like a sports star after a big game. That is until their delusions become completely annoying and sad and it goes on too long. I was dating this girl that had an old friend named Rosalee that was always trying to sleep with her. It was pathetic. Not only did Rosalee look like an absolute troll and

Katie Moran

have no respect for our relationship—she would ask my girlfriend to sleep in bed with her and her husband over and over again—but she would look at my girlfriend all goo-goo eyed as if they were in love. My girlfriend would look at me, and we would laugh in disgust at Rosalee's behavior.

Rosalee thought there was chemistry between the two of them but she was the only one feeling it. My girlfriend did not even like Rosalee to touch her as she would always hold on way too long and put her hands in strategically sexual places. From the way Rosalee closed her eyes and the geeky smile across her face, I could tell she was clearly the only one benefiting from this supposed attraction. Rosalee never snapped out of it. Every time we would visit her she would do the same thing, just to get shot down each and every time. And when she was on the outs with her husband, she would invite herself over to stay at my girlfriend's house and insist on sleeping in our bed. My dog was even more mortified than I was.

After five minutes of Rosalee pretending she was falling asleep while watching television, my dog Soda stuck her black hairy ass in Rosalee's face, stretched out her enormous legs and pushed Rosalee to the floor. Some people call an asshole a "chocolate starfish." When Soda really hates someone or is mad at them she stamps them with her chocolate starfish. A starfish stamp from Soda is definitely not a high compliment. Rosalee ignored the insult and tried one last time to crawl back up and spoon my girlfriend, and that is when I shook her awake and let her know that the futon was made up for her in the other room. Nothing fazes her and her one-sided chemistry remains intact still today. This is a true chemical imbalance.

Of course, the preferred attraction is "true chemistry." True chemistry is mutual attraction. This is the spark that starts the relationship, spurs it forward, and helps keep people together through the years. Mutual sexual chemistry is really like a magical potion that makes the blood boil and livens up all of the senses. It is that moment when you talk to someone for the first time but it feels like you have known him forever. I have chemistry with all of my friends, otherwise we would have run out of things to talk about and lost interest in the friendship long ago.

There are certain members of my family that I have chemistry with and would probably choose to spend time with even if they were not related to me. My Aunt Julia has a heart of gold; I always have a blast with her. Then there are the relatives who are just plain hard work; the ones with whom I have to really struggle to find a common bond while sitting next to them at a wedding or other occasion. It is no one's fault; it is just that the two of us do not click on that inexplicable level that involves so many aspects of personality, age, needs, interest, etc.

I was with a girl named Ruby and it was not working out. The first time we kissed was four weeks into the thing and she started laughing uncontrollably and then cried. When this happened I realized that our relationship was not going anywhere. She claims the failure of the relationship was because she is too spiritual for me; I claim it is because she is one of the most emotionally unavailable women I have ever met. Ruby is still single and I hope she meets the man or woman she is longing for; but I fear that when he finds her she will be locked away alone in her apartment, too busy writing poetry or shuffling tarot cards to let him in.

No one falls in love by staying at home and staying physically and emotionally closed off from the world. My other friends are not so kind to Ruby; they claim that she does get out but just chooses the wrong people to get out with. When Ruby isn't at home she is going to tearooms and spiritual bookstores with "crusty girls." Crusty girls are girls who complain all the time about being single, who are usually in their thirties and complain about that, too. Inevitably, one of the girls in the group is a tackle box. All crusty girl groups must include at

Katie Moran

least one with an offensive pussy. Having a tackle box girl in your group of friends is sure to ward off all potential boyfriends. If she was my friend and I was the first to find that stinky fact out (which one of my guy friends did quite accidentally with the help of a six-pack of Coronas), I would have dragged her to the bathroom, washcloth in hand, and remedied the situation myself.

While Ruby was busy hanging out with the crusty girls, I sat at home writing and trying to figure out how to tape Oprah while watching Seinfeld when they were both on re-runs simultaneously late at night. My phone was ringing over and over again but when I looked at the caller ID it was never Ruby. It would be a fuck buddy wanting to know if I wanted to "rent a movie," or a friend asking if I wanted to go down the street to pick up some food. Yeah, just what I wanted, sex on my fuck buddy's couch and over-eating, not a combination that was going to make me feel any better. Night after night, after turning down several requests to go out and do things that paled in comparison to watching Angelina Jolie in *Gia* yet another time, I succumbed to my friend Patty's invite to go see a band play down the street.

When Patty called, and she heard my less-than-enthusiastic "Yeah?" after the last ring, she said, "You have to stop this bullshit; it's been over a month. Get over it already."

I was on to her. "You don't have anyone to go with you to this lame thing, do you?"

She replied, "I'll drive and I'll pay."

I thought about it for a moment and decided that a drink might be nice and that Angelina could wait for another night. "All right, but no more than two hours." She quickly spit out a "See you at ten" before I could change my mind. I had a long time to get ready because Patty lived on the other side of Highland Ave., which meant she had to drive through Hollywood Bowl traffic.

I would rather shoot myself in the foot than drive through a bunch of freaks trying to find parking and cram into the arena in time for another slow death-by-symphony to begin. It can take up to an hour to get through a tenth of a mile. I knew it was a big geek night over there because some foreign sitar player was in town. In fact I actually like the sitar. It was probably a night of brass. Or cello. Oh just use your imagination, it all sounds the damn same to me and creates horrible traffic. I have trouble staying awake to music with no words.

The point is, as I waited for Patty to arrive I managed to pull myself together and look halfway decent; Patty showed up and was impressed. The goal of the evening was to get me out of the house and to find her a new woman—I was not looking. Plus, I was in a bad mood that night and trying to stay away from any guy that could potentially irritate me in the future. And since this club was filled with aspiring rock stars, I knew it was not the time or the place to troll for cock. The band was actually really good and rocked so hard that it put me in a good mood; I actually forgot that I had hated my life earlier that day. I threw down a couple of Diet Cokes and excused myself to go to the bathroom. I swung open the door and standing in front of me was the most gorgeous girl I had ever seen. She was noted as one of the most beautiful women in the world but here she was, standing in front of a bathroom mirror naked and topless looking right at me.

For a few seconds I experienced something that rarely happens to me; I was at a total loss for words. I could only feel that my eyes were a bit dry from not blinking for too long. She was tall, blonde, blue eyed, and tan with perfect breasts, and just as startled as I was. She did nothing to hide her nakedness. She looked right at me and smiled a perfectly straight white smile and said with a Texas drawl, "I am sooooo sorry! I didn't think anyone was comin' in!"

Katie Moran

I recovered quickly and said, "That's okay, I was actually just about to ask you what you were doing later."

She smiled, appreciating the humor and said, "Well, you're my kind of girl. Later is too far away . . . come over here now!" It was instant chemistry and we made out right there in the bathroom. Her friend flushed a toilet and stepped out of the stall, breaking up our kiss. My blonde put her new shirt on, a baby blue cut-off with the logo of the band that we were all there seeing. I was disappointed to see those breasts disappear behind the taut curtain of cloth but my heart was beating too fast to really care. She grabbed my hand and led me out of the bathroom like her little pet kitten. I felt submissive and that was a fun change from feeling depressed.

Patty spotted me with my gorgeous new find and so did every guy in the joint. Patty's face crinkled up and I could see her mouthing a distinctive, "UUMPH!" from across the room. I just shrugged. I still had not absorbed it all myself. The band had a break and I found out the girl's name, Nadia. She made sure I had a matching shirt with the band's name on it but mine was pink instead of blue. She helped me into it and we kissed again, this time I was able to fondle one of those breasts, trying to determine its authenticity. She asked me what I did and she said, "Well, what a coincidence! You've written for *Playboy* and I've been in *Playboy*!"

She didn't look completely familiar though; she still had some darker blonde tones in her hair. I said, "Were you a Playmate?"

And she said, "Oh heavens no! I am Miss Hawaiian Tropic! We had a spread in there."

I was living out the ultimate male fantasy, standing next to a Hawaiian Tropic girl who had made it clear she was interested in me. Nadia was just as sweet as she was beautiful and we instantly hit it off. She asked me if I thought her boobs were real. I not-so-discreetly reached out to touch them. They looked and felt real; in fact they were absolutely impressive. Nadia went on to explain that her father had given her a set of implants for her eighteenth birthday (my dad had given me a free oil change at Jiffy Lube for my birthday so I couldn't relate) but that they were saline and looked too big and fake. So she had them switched out for the less-popular, and more dangerous, silicone that looked and felt like real breasts. I was careful from then on not to squeeze too hard. Nadia and I had a great night together; our connection was intense and electric. She was dating one of the musicians in the band but when she introduced me to him it was obvious that she had free reign to do whatever she wanted with women.

Right from the start I could sense that there was something off about Nadia but I chose to ignore it because she was so beautiful and so much fun. I knew there was no future for us in anything other than just a great time. As the night went on I noticed that she had a slight sniffing problem so I asked her if she did coke or something. Nadia looked a little embarrassed and admitted that she had a little habit that she was trying to kick but that she was not on anything that night. I have had my run with drugs so I am a good judge of someone's toxicity. She was definitely just drunk that night we met at the club. How drunk? Well, when she signed her bar tab it was two hundred dollars! She was buying a few drinks for friends here and there but the majority of the tab belonged to her. And this was not one of those fifteen-dollar martini bars; she wracked up that bill one three-dollar Heineken and one six-dollar Absolut cran at a time.

Nadia invited me to another club down on Sunset in Holly-wood, east of Vine; one of my friends owned the place so I felt comfortable going there. At this point, I would have felt com-fortable getting on a plane and going just about anywhere with this chick. Nadia and her pal were kind enough to extend the invitation to my friend Patty but she opted to go home. As Patty

Katie Moran

walked out the door she looked back at me, both smiling and shaking her head in disbelief. Nadia and I climbed in the back of a big Cadillac Escalade SUV and things heated up before the car was even in drive. By the time we arrived at the next club, Nadia's pants were lost somewhere between the cargo space we were in and the back seat her friends were sitting in. It was one wild ride and that was only the beginning.

The night at the club was just as fun. All the girls were making out with the members of the band I was with and then turning around and fondling each other. It was a true rocker's night out. I have heard tales of trashed hotel rooms and cancelled tour dates due to excessive partying, groupie drama, and, of course, group sex, and this was one of those nights where I truly let it all hang out. I was with this insane group of hardcore partiers and I was accepted as one of them with open arms and open legs. But Nadia was definitely the catch of the century and the reason why I was there.

When the club ended for the night at 2 AM (which is L.A.'s way of saying to the rest of the world "We suck, don't move here"), we were treated to the ultimate celebrity perk—the after party. My buddy left the club open for the band and all the rest of us to do whatever we wanted to. Now the party really got wild. The drummer was having sex with his girlfriend in one of the booths and another girl decided to take off her pants and hop right on top of the drummer's exposed dick, nudging his girlfriend's mouth out of way with her perfect ass. There was the constant flow of alcohol and drugs, but that seemed incidental to the great music and fantastic company. Everyone was having a spectacular time.

The lead singer informed us all that there was a party going on back at his house and he needed to be there because people were waiting for us. I loved that he considered our night out as a giant group effort. We showed up at his house and it was truly like a clip from one of those behind-the-music type shows. There were bottles and cans everywhere—I would estimate at least a thousand empties in a three-thousand-square-foot house. There was music blasting rock 'n' roll from floor-to-ceiling speakers and beautiful men and women hanging out on every surface. I mingled with the partygoers until I was summoned to the guesthouse by Nadia. We aggressively took advantage of each other for several hours. She fell off the bed not once, but twice, due to her intoxication. In all honesty, the sex was not all that gratifying because she would be fervently suctioned to my inner thigh thoroughly convinced that it was a clitoris.

The adrenaline of the entire evening more than made up for it. Sometimes atmosphere can change the entire dynamic of a sexual encounter for me. The aesthetics of this beautiful model were enough to make any man cum through the ceiling. I was more focused on making sure that she did just that. Nadia admittedly had not been with anyone as skilled as me. I usually do not toot my own horn but I owe it all to being only half as trashed as she was. The shock of her orgasm sent her soaring backward into the headboard, eyes squinted closed and mouth wide open. She muttered an "I love you" and I smiled with pride. Her boyfriend sat back and watched in admiration. As much as I am a girl who appreciates the beauty of monogamy and intimacy, I still can understand the erotic effects of voyeurism.

Nadia reluctantly drove me home at seven in the morning after we finished fooling around. She drove around in circles, ignoring the annoying voice of her navigation system telling her where to turn. She passed my street and confessed that she did not want me to leave. I was flattered and touched, to say the least. We shared a cigarette and sat in her car for an hour before I went back into my house, greeted by my maniacal dog who wanted to know every detail and investigated the answers for herself, by sniffing my crotch and face repeatedly.

Katie Moran

I did not take the night with Nadia as a sign of incredible chemistry. I basically chalked it up to a chemical imbalance. The combination of alcohol and atmosphere tipped the scales of what would normally occur in nature. I thought if she and I had met at the Coffee Bean on a Sunday afternoon we would have passed each other with nothing more than a smile and maybe a wink. But, due to the amount of alcohol she had consumed and due to the effects that great music had on our senses and our body chemistry, a force of desperate and searching attraction threw us together.

Surprisingly enough, Nadia called me the next day to tell me what an incredible time she had with me and how she could not wait to spend time with me again. I was so shocked that I drove over to Bobby's house to play the message to him. I showed him her bikini photos on the Internet and he gasped with glee. "Oh honey, she is FABULOUS! She makes Ruby look like a dirty old skank! Congrats!"

Nadia and I went out again the next week and it turned out to be a toned-down version of our first night together. It was a lot of fun but I still did not really know who she was. I got a glimpse of her past; her strained relationship with her father, her battles in and out of rehab, her sister's life as a stripper; her upbringing as a Texas debutante, and mostly her desire to be with the same sex. All of this is the making of an LA party girl. I felt that Nadia looked at me as some sort of savior because, although I was only a couple years older than she, I had been there, done that, and recovered from it all, especially when it came to drugs and alcohol. But I had already been with "this" girl. Running around with Kristina had been like this and I was not willing to go back to a life that could only be compared to walking the razor's edge.

I offered Nadia my friendship but I could tell she was not ready to deal with the emotional pains that were bothering her. She couldn't become my friend because it was too hard for her to stay sober long enough to let me know who she really was. I saw her a few more times, once when she called me drunk on Thanksgiving Day because she would rather spend the night in a bar with me than with her family in Texas. I found her lifestyle heartbreaking. The last time I saw her was at another wild party. I ran into her and she seemed really coked up. She said she had broken up with her boyfriend and wanted to spend more time with me. I blamed the chemicals for her over-abundance of emotion toward me. I never discouraged her; I just smiled and gave her a big hug and a passionate kiss. I told her she could call whenever she wanted to talk to me. I never heard from her again.

Shortly after that last encounter with Nadia I moved out of the city to do some traveling and changed my number. I will probably never know what would have happened if I had let myself love this woman but I suspect it would have been messy. After several failed relationships and too much experience chasing uncertain people, I was not willing to put my heart on the line to find out. Nadia is definitely one of those people that I will always think about and wonder where she is and how she is doing, hoping she has given up the drugs completely and found something that made her really happy or someone who showed her an incredible amount of compassion. Nadia will also go down in my history as one gorgeous girl who turned me on and sent my life on an amazing ride for a brief moment in time.

Then there are those people you date who are interesting and great and funny, perfect in every single way, but just do nothing to turn you on. The ones that make you feel like you might as well be on a date with your grandma. It is nobody's fault, but it happens all the time. Then I find myself coming up with a thousand different diplomatic ways to subtly indicate to my date that he or she repels me. The worst is when they want to see you again and you have to find a way to politely excuse yourself from this person's life forever. Have you ever been on a date with someone who is nice, smart, funny, and good looking but you sit through the entire conversation wondering, "Why am I not attracted to this person?"

After I broke up with Danny and he moved back east (do they all have to go so far to get away from me?), I went on a date with this blond music exec named Bret that I met through an Internet personal. I have found out the hard way that guys are far more deceitful than women when it comes to how they present themselves in personal ads. However, Bret looked so sexy in his photo—reporting that he was six feet tall and looking all handsome and rugged in a dashing cowboy hat—that I decided to give him a chance. Warning: When a guy wears a hat in a photo it is probably because he is bald. Or, as in Bret's case, he is getting to be bald and getting there fast. Bret showed up at the restaurant and he turned out to be super sweet, but he and his three hairs were barely standing above five foot seven.

Okay, so Bret was a liar but he was also a nice person and I really wanted to like him. He had all the makings of a good boyfriend, but the thought of him touching me made me want to duct tape my breasts, dress in a full body suit of dog hair, and top it off with a nun's habit and a piece of skunk-juice-sprayed notebook paper taped to my face that read "Hell no!" Instead, I let him kiss me. I guess I was hoping that something would change. I was wrong. I pulled away from him and ducked into my car quickly. I grabbed the closest item, a sweatshirt, and proceeded to spit in it and wipe my mouth until my lips were nearly raw. Dramatic? I suppose so. The extremity of my behavior was inexplicable. Bret was perfect relationship material and yet I could never sleep with him in a million years. The final words on chemistry . . . when it's not there, it's just not there.

8

Truth Is Stranger
Than Fiction

exual deviancy is relative; what one person finds atrocious another may find routine. In order to properly dissect this subject a book would have to cover each and every fetish, individual indiscretion, practice, or obsession, and yes, I would love to read such a book! Sexual deviancy includes any type of detour from "the norm," something different than what people are doing in their bedrooms day in and day out. These are things that are brow-raising to the average person and may be taken as a step toward sexual and personal exploration or just digested as a good story. I have chosen a few experiences

Originally appeared in *Playboy Magazine.*

to highlight some of the more colorful moments. This is a very tiny part of a much larger culture.

The Sex Club

I was offended when my friend Seth—a guy that I date casually—invited me to a sex club. "A swingers' club? Isn't that for old trashy couples looking to spice up their fizzled-out sex lives?" He said no, and that a lot of young people are going to them to try new things, like multiple partners or exhibitionism. He found out about it through an Internet invite linked to a Web site.

Most swingers' clubs have Web sites, and they require a picture to be submitted before adding you to their guest list. In major cities they are easy to find—they are listed in the back of weekly newspapers and can be found by doing searches on the Internet. They are often called swinger's parties, lust clubs, fuck bars, erotic shows; you name it. At a true swingers' club, only couples and single women are allowed to go. I suppose it's to keep out the sexual predators—aka sleazy single men.

The club we went to had a theme for different nights of the week. Of course, my date and I had no idea what the theme was ahead of time but it was painfully obvious once we showed up that it was porn night. Like most of these "establishments," the club was way out in suburbia, in a seedy part of town about twenty minutes from Hollywood. We walked in and it appeared to be a normal strip club. We felt like the virginal straight couple from hell, dressed conservatively compared to the sparkling mess of sex outfits strewn on half-naked bodies. I suggest that you find out the theme or dress code beforehand and dress as sexy and hot as you possibly can. After all, it is no secret as to what everyone is there for. The beauty of a sex club is that there is no hidden agenda.

At this club, to set the mood, there was a huge dance floor and two stages with poles on which gorgeous girls were dancing topless. There were booths around the back and side where couples were sitting and drinking. The place was big and had the feel of a seventies underground disco—not that I've ever been to one, but that's what it felt like. It all looked pretty tame to me, but it was early.

Seth and I took a walk to the back, the VIP room, where we assumed most of the action would take place. Only one couple was having sex back there. I danced for a while, my eyes wandering around looking for sexual acts taking place. There were some of the hottest people there I had ever seen, including some well-known porn stars dressed in glitter and gold. This place appeared to be where the sex industry goes for fun. The club caters to the skin trade and lots of strippers and their boyfriends go there on dates. Seth's dentist was there too, with his wife, who is also the receptionist at his office. All types swing, I decided.

About an hour later, at midnight, there were about ten girls on the stage and six were dancing on the bar, completely nude, touching each other and kissing passionately. I noticed guys getting blowjobs in the booths in the main room. My date and I were like kids in a candy store, running from one end of the room to the other to check out the action. One girl had shaved her pussy hair into polka dots and dyed it green.

Then I heard "What the hell are you doing here?" come at me from the back. It was my ex-girlfriend, Jasmine, the wild girl who loved to drink. We had been on the outs for some time but I guess she was no longer mad at me for calling her a dirty whore (I was joking, but English is her second language, so she didn't get it). I thought at first that we could overcome our differences and overcome our inhibitions in a place like the sex club. Basically, I just wanted to get some. I am sure my date would have appreciated it—he was staring at us, his eyes darting back and forth, probably forming a mental image of the two of us engaged in a 69. But Jasmine had turned into a stiff in this

Katie Moran

place. The whole time at the club, she didn't even take her coat off. "Closet case," I thought to myself. I ditched her on the patio. I was far more interested in the dynamics surrounding me than whether or not her tongue would be somewhere on my body that night.

The key to a swingers' club is to meet people early in the evening, start talking and make friends. These are people that you may want to hook up with later so it is good to get to know them and have them feel comfortable with you first. Otherwise, you will be left like we were, in the main room, dodging the gazes of ugly couples who everyone else had left for broke. Seth and I had been having so much fun dancing and spying that we almost missed the action . . . almost.

By 1 AM the place was in full swing. Couples and threesomes were going at it in the VIP room in these little red vinyl booths usually meant for lap dances. I jumped up on stage and was stroking this beautiful blond chick's ass—she was wearing a dress hiked up to her navel and no panties and swinging on one of the many poles. Women were now laid flat on their backs on the stages, while men were in front of them performing oral sex. A few times I saw a row of people going down on each other, five or six deep. Men with their asses shaved looked like women from the backside; there was just skin and sweat everywhere.

The back room was my favorite, all dark and steamy, gently illuminated by a red glow from a single light in the corner. By 1:30 everyone had piled to the back, in groups of two, three, four, and five. But, from my perspective, everyone looked united, as one. It was the most easily accessible orgy around. All that I could hear was panting and a cooperative moan and the sound was such a turn on. The little Spanish girl I had been eyeing the whole night had already teamed up with the married couple in the cowboy hats when my date and I decided to jump in. We grabbed a booth and went at it. We positioned ourselves so that we could see everyone else and so I could reach over the back of the booth and kiss this hot girl covered in pink sequins. It was amazing. Just hot, urgent sex. The club closed at 2 AM, but the bouncers were nice enough to let anyone who wanted to finish up stay until 3.

I think sex clubs are a safe way to explore your sexuality and they are much more fun than a hotel room.

The Masseuse

A doctor puts patients in a compromising position every day. For a doctor who has a very dominant personality, this relationship can increase their feeling of being in a position of power. A patient has to trust the hands of a doctor not to hurt them when they are lying there, naked, exposed, and vulnerable. I know a woman, my friend Roberta, who is very submissive. She makes monthly appointments to see her doctor, a gynecologist, even when there is nothing physically wrong with her. She admits to getting off by being in a prone position, on a cold table, fondled by an older man while in a sterile environment.

My friend Vanessa is a surgeon. Every day her patients lie on a table before her, unconscious and unknowing as she cuts into their bodies, delicately cutting and stitching their organs . . . Her hands delve deep into their tissues, exposing layers of flesh and pints of blood. Vanessa enjoys her work but eventually she began to crave something with a little more sensuality. Unlike Roberta, Vanessa found nothing sexy about the doctor/patient relationship. Roberta gets off from any type of medical fantasy and spends quite a bit of money purchasing nurse's uniforms, speculums, syringes, plastic tubing, enemas, gauze, and almost anything else found in a doctor's office. Vanessa, on the other hand, searched for a sensual outlet to wield her position of power. I was surprised when she told me she was going to massage school.

"Why are you taking massage? You work sixteen-hour days

Katie Moran

and make $400,000 a year. When are you going to have time to give massages?"

Vanessa, never one to explain anything, said, "It just sounds like fun."

I met Vanessa at a time in her life when she was having serious marital problems. Her husband, a Wall Street banker, had been ignoring her to the point that it would be considered abusive. He was out every night and would come home after she had fallen asleep. If she would wake up and try to say hi to him she was met with nothing more than a scowl. After months of mistreatment and her begging him to seek help with no results, she sought the attention of another romantic interest, me. However, I was not interested in her. Perhaps I sensed she was in a messy relationship or maybe I was not attracted to her other than as a friend. She pursued other women as an escape from her marriage but failed to find someone to date. She gave up and vowed to dedicate her time to her career. Well, she went through with the massage school despite criticism from her colleagues, who thought she might be over-extending herself. She fell in love with massaging clients and it became a healthy outlet for her for quite a while. She was working too many hours, though, just as suspected by her peers. She did not want to give up surgery or massage, but she needed some time to herself. For a mini escape, whenever she had a chance she would book a relaxing massage for herself at one of the most exclusive spas in Los Angeles.

She had been seeing the same massage therapist once a week for three months. Her masseuse, a blond, blue-eyed German with the looks and physique of an underwear model, impressed Vanessa, who was a tall African-American woman with striking features. His name was Ben. Soon Vanessa found herself equally impressed by his massage skills and the incredibly sexy demeanor he had with his clients. She looked forward to taking her clothes off and lying naked on a massage table, exposing herself to this attractive man, and being caressed by his capable hands. It was the attention that she had been wanting for the past year from her absentee husband. She continued seeing him and admitted to me that she had developed a crush on him. Vanessa gathered that most of his female clients were probably smitten with him. Why not? He was gorgeous and he was touching them in a way that made them feel good.

One day Vanessa was particularly tired after getting off a twenty-four-hour shift at the hospital. She went to see Ben and started to drift into sleep on his table. About half an hour into the massage, while she was in a relaxed and dreamy state, eyes flickering with exhaustion, Vanessa's massage took a turn into the peculiar. As Ben rubbed his strong hands down Vanessa's backside and over the curve of her ass, he gently spread her thin legs to reveal her wet vagina. He slipped two fingers inside of her, massaging the walls of her vagina and her G spot just as he would the rest of her body. It took her thirty seconds before she fully awoke and realized what was going on. She had no time (and no energy) to decide whether Ben's actions were a violation or not. Instead she closed her eyes and let him bring her to full orgasm. What he did next was a shocker. Ben yanked down his shorts and masturbated himself fervently over Vanessa's naked body. He pushed his cock up against her ass and proceeded to ejaculate all over her back, rubbing it in like massage oil. This is what finally pried her tired eyes open to the size of saucers. She asked him kindly to clean her off before she returned home to her husband.

Vanessa kept her appointment with Ben the next week, never giving him a higher tip than the time before. She returned week after week for two months solid to receive the same treatment, sometimes having up to five orgasms. After the first time, Ben came into a towel. He must have sensed that the ejaculation made her uncomfortable. I speculated that Vanessa's continuation of this behavior had more to do with submission than just the need for sexual and emotional attention that was lacking in

Katie Moran

121

her marriage. It was role reversal. Vanessa was a surgeon, a woman used to taking a power position with her patients. She admitted the stress of her job had taken over, and she would never have succumbed to Ben's strange and inappropriate advances otherwise. She was now the one on the operating table, exposed and defenseless. She was being penetrated by Ben's hands instead of by a scalpel. In her exhausted state of mind, the two worlds had blurred together. The way to escape from her position of dominance was to slip into submission.

Vanessa continued her strange affair with Ben until things became even weirder than they already were. Her masseuse started to grow jealous of her marriage and the fact that she was still in it. He said they should not continue doing what they were doing in the spa any longer. Feeling like an open wound about to burst through its sutures, Vanessa asked Ben the question that had been swelling inside of her for weeks . . . "If I were single would you be interested in me?" He responded in an unexpected and insulting way, saying, "You are a beautiful woman and I would love to continue doing this to you if you weren't married. But only on the table." She called me, upset and feeling the exploitation most women would have felt the moment he invaded her that very first day. As we talked through her experience, I could tell she was trying to make sense of the whole encounter. I told Vanessa that Ben was probably nothing more than a prostitute with a high-priced location in a spa instead of in a hotel room. When she replied that Ben had told her that he had never done that before, I laughed and told her that people lie. Some people are crazy and other people lie, just like she had lied to her husband about having a sixty-year-old female masseuse all this time.

The Vehicle

I have slept in beds all over the world in pursuit of hot sex but the strangest place I have ever slept was not so hot at all. One night I had met this really great guy and we totally hit it off. We dated for a few weeks before we had sex which was wonderful, not the best I had ever had but definitely up to par. One night he brought me aboard a beautiful yacht in Marina del Rey. We got our groove on in a romantic cabin aboard the boat complete with champagne and music playing. The next night we fucked in the back of a military Humvee. Over the weekend, we were at a large harbor having sex on a different boat. I questioned him and he could not come up with a straight answer as to how he had access to all of these interesting locations. I asked him if we could maybe spend the evening at my place, relaxing in front of the fireplace or having sex in my extremely comfortable bedroom. He looked at me in disgust. This was my first sign that he was not a "normal" kind of guy. I am always up for a little adventure and excitement, but always when balanced with something familiar and comfortable. I like a night on the run but I also equally enjoy a night spent at home. He saw it differently.

I played along with his shenanigans until one night his secret was revealed. He took me onboard a yacht with the name *Sandy and Tyler* carefully painted across the back of the boat. Now, this guy's name was neither Sandy nor Tyler and this boat was far too impressive to belong to any of his friends—I realized we had been breaking into cars and boats all along. These must have been locations he had been to many times before because he did not have to break any locks. The Humvee was a convertible so it was wide open, and the yacht door was unlocked. In one case he actually had a key. I cannot enjoy sex when I am scared and once I had realized what was happening the fun was over for me. I was young but I also knew that an armed soldier probably would not be too thrilled to find us in the back of his vehicle. I asked my date to drop me off at a friend's home in a nearby beach town.

It was three in the morning when we pulled up in front of my

Katie Moran

friend's condo; I was pretty sure she would be home and the guy dropped me off and drove away before confirming I had entered the condo. I quickly realized I had a problem; my friend's car was there but she was not answering the phone. I found out later that she had taken an Ambien and passed out, but at that moment all I knew was that I had no car, and I was miles away from a payphone so I could not call a cab. I was so tired I could have cried from exhaustion, so I roamed the condo complex for a safe place to wait until daybreak. I grew desperate and found the only sanctuary, a large van—the perfect end to my strange vehicular sex marathon. I crawled underneath it and fell asleep on the cold concrete, even managing to sleep pretty well considering the circumstances. I did not wake up until I heard the sound of an engine roar up at nine the next morning. I panicked like an inmate on death row walking to the electric chair. I thought it was over for me. I rolled out and jumped to my feet just as a neighboring station wagon rolled backward inches from my feet. I don't think the driver of the car will ever forget the sight of me popping up from under his neighbor's van, wearing a purple halter-top and mini skirt with high heels and in full make-up. He looked like he had seen a ghost or the second coming of Christ. His face turned white and he drove down the alley, stopping frequently to peer in his rearview mirror and crane his neck to look at me.

I never entered my friend's condo but I did manage to hike two miles barefoot (I took the painful party shoes off) to the nearest 7-11 to call a taxi. I could have walked twenty miles with no problem. It was daylight and I was no longer scared. I just wanted to go home and melt into my bed, definitely done with sex, vehicles, and the road for a very long time.

Cindy and Nancy

Nancy, a seventeen-year-old freshman, found the first day of college exciting for many reasons, the most thrilling of which was meeting her roommate for the first time. Nancy arrived at her small freshman dorm room first, choosing the bed on the right side of the room. She was a sheltered girl from a gated community in Northern California who had no siblings and had attended a high school of only ninety-five people. She looked forward to really branching out and meeting new friends. She also looked forward to meeting a boyfriend and maybe losing her virginity.

When eighteen-year-old Cindy opened the door, standing there smelling like Bath and Body Works products and looking like she just finished cheerleading practice, Nancy knew they were kindred spirits. They went out immediately and explored the campus, pointing out all the cute guys that they wanted to flirt with and all the girls they thought they would have to compete with. Later, they took turns taking showers in the small bathroom. Cindy was not shy and dropped her pink towel to the floor, putting lotion on her long legs right in front of shy Nancy, who was taken aback by her blatant immodesty.

After Nancy took a shower, she shyly changed in the closet, only exposing one section at a time to put her clothes on. Just as Nancy had taken off her towel to expose here lower half, Cindy busted in on her. Cindy apologized but offered her some new crème that smelled like hazelnut. Nancy shyly thanked her and tucked herself deeper in the closet to put her panties on.

That night, Cindy and Nancy set their television and DVD player up, attaching all the wires and situating it in a corner. They lay on their separate beds, now freshly decorated with ruffled pillows and clean girlie sheets. They watched Nancy's favorite DVD, *Legally Blonde,* and drifted off to sleep. Just as the movie ended, Nancy heard a crashing sound and the next thing she knew she was on the floor. Her bed had broken! Is this what college was like? Roommates who saw you getting undressed and cheap beds that broke? Nancy was missing home already. Cindy jumped to her rescue, grabbing her arm and

Katie Moran

pulling her up off the floor. The bed was a mess; even the mattress had folded in half. Cindy told Nancy that she would have to share a bed with her. Nancy replied, "No, that's okay. I'll just sleep on the floor."

Cindy said, "Don't be ridiculous. This bed is big enough for the two of us."

"No it's not," Nancy thought. She reluctantly climbed in bed next to Cindy, their bare skin touching.

Nancy could not sleep. Her heart was racing too fast from the shock of her bed breaking. She closed her eyes and realized that Cindy's perfume smelled great. Her tank top and matching boy briefs, which must have come from Victoria's Secret, felt so nice and silky compared to her own flannel pajama pants. "Cindy has to be sleeping already," Nancy thought. She envied her for being so comfortable in this new situation at college. Nancy knew that even if she were in her own bed she would be too nervous to sleep. This whole new life was overwhelming. Nancy wanted to cry. Just then Cindy rolled over and put her petite hand right on top of Nancy's breast! She was horrified. Nancy tried to move it but it was glued there.

Nancy did not want to make a stink and wake Cindy up so she just lay there, feeling awkward. She closed her eyes again and realized something strange was happening to her body. She felt wet, like she had gotten her period, and she thought to herself, "Oh great, I am sleeping in someone else's bed, she has her hand on me, and now THIS happens? What next?" Well, next were Nancy's nipples beginning to stiffen underneath Cindy's palm, which was now curiously moving up and down. Nancy had never felt this way before, except for the one time she watched a dirty movie in eighth grade with her best friend Andrea. She did not want it to end. She felt bad because she knew it was a mistake. She knew that if Cindy woke up she would be shocked and embarrassed.

Or would she . . .

The "On" Position

—————————————————

Nancy looked to her side to find Cindy staring square in her eyes. Nancy couldn't recall what happened in the brief moment before their lips touched; it happened too fast. They kissed each other for what seemed like hours and fell asleep with their hands massaging each other's breasts.

Cindy and Nancy went on to four successful years of college, experiencing much more than what happened that very first night. And they never moved out of the dorms, like so many upperclassmen do. Gee, I wonder why.

The story of Cindy and Nancy, although one of my favorites, is not true. It is a complete scenario of role playing. My ex and I used these two characters to enhance our lovemaking. I was Cindy and she was Nancy. Wherever we went, anywhere across the world, we could bring these two along to make us feel right at home. And when one of us may not have been in the mood for sex, there was always the possibility that Cindy or Nancy would be.

I have a lot of other "characters" that I have used in the past to boost my sex drive. I have broken out the old "the doctor will see you now" routine. I pretend I am undergoing an examination by a really hot (and very inappropriate) female gynecologist. One of my wild characters, a mail-order bride, was so loud in a New Orleans hotel room that we had security called on us by an anal-retentive neighbor. I thought that was completely ridiculous. We were in the Big Easy, after all; and the mail-order bride wasn't *that* loud.

The Comedienne

I know a very sweet guy by the name of Dylan who had a very famous girlfriend. He and I were just becoming friends but I could tell that we had a lot in common. I went to his home quite a bit for parties and small gatherings but his girlfriend was never home because she was on tour with her show. I was a fan of her work and had wanted to interview her for a story. He told me to come to her birthday party the next month to meet her and discuss different publication options for an interview.

Dylan and I e-mailed back and forth and talked on the phone. He was excited because his girlfriend had proposed to him in the back of a limo on the way to a big premiere. She had bought him his dream car, a Porsche, as an engagement gift. Things were going great and I was so happy for him. It seemed like a match made in heaven.

I heard from Dylan about a week before the party and then he kind of disappeared. I thought that he must be really busy with all the birthday preparations; the couple was having over 300 people at their Hollywood Hills home. I brought my boyfriend at the time with me to the party. We saw the guest of honor, whom we barely recognized because she had lost so much weight. We gave her the gift we brought and went outside on the patio. I remarked to my boyfriend how skinny the actress had gotten and how weird she was acting. Her voice sounded forced and high pitched. I figured that people must be much different than they appeared onscreen. We combed the grounds but could not find Dylan anywhere. I asked another party guest where the comedienne's boyfriend was and he pointed to a tall pockmarked man in a monk's outfit. He was creepy, to say the least. Moreover, he definitely wasn't Dylan.

I marched right up to the woman and asked her, "Where is Dylan?" She replied in a creepy, vampire-like voice, "Dylan is no more. He will never step foot in this house again. This is my new boyfriend, Fred." I felt like I was having an out-of-body experience. I knew it was her fault and not Dylan's. Even if Dylan had done something really bad, like cheated on her, there was no way she would have a new boyfriend within one week. I grabbed my boyfriend, plucked my keys out of the valet's hands, and rushed out of there.

I called Dylan the next day. He was in Switzerland. He said

he had to get as far away from his girlfriend as possible because he feared she might end up dead and he did not want to be blamed for it. He said it was over between them. Right after the engagement, she snapped. He walked in their bedroom and found her with Fred, naked and bound in an animalistic way, getting burned with a blowtorch down her back. The room was full of rotting animal carcasses and weird altars. She was screaming in pain and Fred had a full hard on. They looked at innocent Dylan as if he was the intruder.

The movie *Secretary* is one of the best movies to really shed light on the S&M lifestyle. In it, a couple find true love because they understand each other's sexual desires, desires that had previously scared off their other partners. Unlike the characters in *Secretary*, there was nothing funny or loving about what was happening with the comedienne and her boyfriend. It was frightening and sadistic, beyond all measure of sanity. She enjoyed it, got off on it, and continues to practice it still to this day. Her body is permanently scarred from all the burning and cutting inflicted upon her.

The first time I saw a list of all the ways in which domination was played out, I nearly fainted. It was a checklist that an ex-dominatrix friend of mine used to gauge what her clients liked and how much of it they could take.

Some of the more shocking and obscure items on the domination checklist include the following list that I have compiled. Keep in mind that the following list represents only a slight percentage of what is actually practiced:

- ✦ Abrasion
- ✦ Anal plugs
- ✦ Anal plug (in public)
- ✦ Animal roles
- ✦ Asphyxiation
- ✦ Auctioned for charity
- ✦ Ball stretching
- ✦ Bathroom-use control
- ✦ Bestiality
- ✦ Beating
- ✦ Blindfolds
- ✦ Boot worship

Katie Moran

- ✦ Branding
- ✦ Bruises
- ✦ Cages
- ✦ Caning
- ✦ Castration fantasy
- ✦ Catheterization
- ✦ Cattle prod (electrical toy)
- ✦ Cells
- ✦ Chains
- ✦ Chamber-pot use
- ✦ Chastity belts
- ✦ Chauffeuring
- ✦ Choking
- ✦ Chores (maid service)
- ✦ Clothespins
- ✦ Cock worship
- ✦ Corsets
- ✦ Cross-dressing
- ✦ Cuffs (metal or leather)
- ✦ Cutting
- ✦ Diapers
- ✦ Dilation
- ✦ Dildos
- ✦ Double penetration
- ✦ Electro torture
- ✦ Enemas (for punishment)
- ✦ Enforced chastity
- ✦ Exercise (forced/ required)
- ✦ Exhibitionism
- ✦ Eye contact restrictions
- ✦ Face slapping
- ✦ Fantasy abandonment
- ✦ Fantasy rape or gang rape
- ✦ Fear
- ✦ Fisting (anal or vaginal)
- ✦ Flame play
- ✦ Following orders
- ✦ Food deprivation
- ✦ Food play
- ✦ Foot worship
- ✦ Forced bedwetting
- ✦ Forced dressing
- ✦ Forced eating
- ✦ Forced homosexuality
- ✦ Forced heterosexuality
- ✦ Forced masturbation
- ✦ Forced nudity
- ✦ Forced servitude
- ✦ Forced smoking
- ✦ Full head hoods
- ✦ Gags (cloth)
- ✦ Gags (inflatable)
- ✦ Gags (phallic)
- ✦ Gags (rubber)
- ✦ Gags (tape)
- ✦ Gas masks
- ✦ Genital sex
- ✦ Given away to another dom (temporary or permanent)
- ✦ Golden showers
- ✦ Gunplay
- ✦ Hairbrush spankings
- ✦ Hair pulling

- Hand jobs (giving)
- Hand jobs (receiving)
- Harems
- Harnesses
- Having food chosen
- Having clothing chosen
- High heel wearing
- High heel worship
- Homage with tongue (non-sexual)
- Hoods
- Hot oils (on genitals)
- Hot waxing
- Human puppy dog
- Humiliation (private)
- Humiliation (public)
- Hypnotism
- Ice cubes
- Immobilization
- Infantilism
- Initiation rites
- Injections
- Intricate (Japanese) rope bondage
- Interrogations
- Kidnapping
- Kneeling
- Knife play
- Leather clothing
- Leather restraints
- Lectures for misbehavior
- Lingerie (men)
- Manacles and irons
- Manicures (giving)
- Medical scenes
- Modeling for erotic photos
- Mouth bits
- Mummification
- Name change (temporary)
- Name change (legal, permanent)
- Nipple clamps
- Nipple weights
- Oral/anal play (rimming)
- Over-the-knee spanking
- Orgasm denial
- Pain (mild)
- Pain (medium)
- Pain (severe)
- Persona training
- Personality modification
- Phone sex
- Piercing (temporary)
- Piercing (permanent)
- Plastic surgery
- Prison scenes
- Prostitution (public pretense)
- Prostitution (actual)
- Pony slave
- Public exposure
- Punishment scene
- Pussy/cock whipping
- Pussy worship
- Riding crops

- Riding the "horse" (crotch torture)
- Rituals
- Religious scenes
- Restrictive rules on behavior
- Rubber/latex clothing
- Rope body harness
- Saran wrapping
- Scarification
- Scratching—getting
- Scratching—giving
- Sensory deprivation
- Serving as art
- Serving as ashtray
- Serving as furniture
- Serving as toilet (urine)
- Serving as toilet (feces)
- Serving as waitress/waiter
- Sexual deprivation (short term)
- Sexual deprivation (long term)
- Shaving
- Skinny dipping
- Sleep deprivation
- Sleep sacks
- Spandex clothing
- Spanking
- Speech restrictions
- Speculums (anal or vaginal)
- Spitting
- Spreader bars
- Standing in corner
- Stocks
- Straight jackets
- Strap-on dildos
- Strapping (full body beating)
- Suspension (upright)
- Suspension (inverted)
- Suspension (horizontal)
- Swallowing feces
- Swallowing semen
- Swallowing urine
- Tampon training (in ass)
- Tattooing
- Tickling
- Triple penetration
- Uniforms
- Verbal humiliation
- Water torture
- Waxing
- Weight gain (forced)
- Weight loss (forced)
- Whips

As you can see, there are plenty of ways to explore your freaky side. My friend Bobby has many claims to fame, like drinking the most Dr. Peppers and smoking the most Salems in one car ride across Hollywood. One notable claim to fame of Bobby's is his ability to help people find their inner freak. He says he can pull a freak out of anyone. Maybe you have a friend like that, someone who dares you to try something different, to wear that pink boa and that crazy cowboy hat to a club or to have another dance with that one guy who already told you how he likes to have his hair pulled. One night Bobby came out of the bathroom of a club we were at and handed me a balled-up black leather string. He asked me, "Could you hold this for me. It was killing my balls."

I forced it back into his hand and screamed, "Eew! I can't believe you tried to make me hold your cock ring!"

Good for Bobby for trying it out, even if it did chafe his nuts all night. Maybe you are not lucky enough to have a friend like Bobby or maybe you *are* a friend like Bobby! In any case, there is no right or wrong way to explore the unknown, just make sure your method is safe and does not hurt another person . . . unless they beg for it!

Katie Moran

9

Little Dick Eyes

How do you know the size of a man's penis without seeing it? It's in the eyes. My friends and I have created a surefire system to determine the length and girth of a man's member before actually having to take the plunge into the unknown. But first, let's discuss the topic of size. Does size really matter? I think so. Any woman who says otherwise is just being polite or sticking up for her boyfriend's less-than-Tommy Lee–sized cock.

I have been with plenty of men, all shapes, sizes, and colors. The two men I dated the longest, my only real boyfriends, both measured eight inches, but I have found pleasure with as little as six. Your feelings can affect your perception of size; I was surprised to find out that a guy I had been dating for a year had a six-inch cock. His dick seemed large and downright perfect to me. This particular guy never felt the need to lie about it; but I know that most men lie—or at least the men I have been with did. The other guys I dated who said they measured in at six inches were really only about four inches. I can't really be mad at them—if I were a guy, I would probably bump it up an inch too. I have been lying about my weight for years and I think a lot of women do. I figure no one is going to know if I just round it down about three pounds. Maybe that is what men think—that no one will find out.

Many people claim that race has a lot to do with penis size. The race determination of size is really just a generalization. I would not say that race is a guarantee of size by any means; a black man can have a small dick while an Asian man can unzip and reveal a third arm. But, in my experience, I have never seen anything but the stereotype. However, my friends have seen it all.

One friend Kisha was dating an African-American man named Edward. She called me from her cell phone really late one night after leaving Edward's house. She couldn't stop laughing; she said his dick was the size of her middle finger. When I told her I felt bad for Edward she said I should feel bad for *her*. I think that having a small penis is a sensitive subject for many men, straight or gay, and should be treated as such. That does not mean you should stay with someone who cannot satisfy you sexually.

I set my friend Bobby up with a really sweet guy named Peter, a bartender friend of mine. I thought they would make a perfect couple. Peter was really taken with Bobby and was so excited about their newly formed relationship. Their affair finally went to the next level and, just as soon as it began, it was over. Peter called me and he was absolutely crestfallen. I knew the reason why before he told me. I had made a horrible error in my matchmaking. Bobby, although possessing an average-sized dick himself, was a major size queen. He loves big and beautiful dick.

I sort of figured Peter as a small-penised kind of guy. He had soft eyes that looked longingly into your soul like a sick kitten. He lacked confidence. I wanted so much for him to find love; but in the gay world, it is hard to find someone willing to date a thirty-seven-year-old who has lost his boyish charm but still has his boy-sized weenie. Peter painfully recounted the evening's events. They went out to dinner; went back to Bobby's place, Peter blew Bobby, and then Bobby saw Peter's dick. And that was the end of it.

My next phone call was to Bobby. I knew he would not call me; he was avoiding me because he did not want to 'fess up to his size discrimination. He repeated something to me that I had heard several times before, "Honey, I don't fuck ugly. And that was one ugly little dick!" So, not only was it not big but it was not pretty either.

Jasmine dated a guy for about a year that had a huge coke-can-sized penis. Unfortunately, he had the temper to match— he was an absolute nightmare. He ruined her credit, committed insurance fraud under her name, smacked her around a couple of times, and kicked dents in her new car. He was a bad person and no matter how big of a member he had, she did not want anything to do with him after his inexcusable behavior. If it had been up to me he would be sharing his big dick with some new mates down on Cell Block 10. Jasmine found a new guy that all of her friends approved of. He was a sweetheart of a guy who stayed at home to take care of his mom and grandmother. He was an actor, but the kind who actually worked. Jasmine was madly in love with him and had known him since high school. I wanted them to be together more than anything.

I thought they would make such a great couple. Jasmine knew her new guy would not be as well endowed as her criminal ex, but she did not care. She said she would think of the new guy when she was masturbating and cum in thirty seconds. The first night she had sex with him was amazing. She said she closed her eyes and dreamed of him inside of her and when she opened her eyes and saw his gorgeous face, she realized that her dream was real and she was living it. The intensity of their love was orgasmic on its own.

When it comes to friends and talking about sex, we both agree that it is not real until you tell someone about it. So naturally Jasmine called me first thing in the morning (noon, that is) and insisted on coming over to re-hash her night of romance. She told me how great it was to finally be with him after all these years and she repeated all the wonderful things he said to her, about how special she was, how great he felt when he was around her, and how waiting for the moment that they would have sex made the actual sex all the better. I wanted to know the good stuff, "How big is he?" She asked me where my bag of sex toys was and I pointed to the closet.

She sifted through the masses of color and size, taking out a few to admire. Finally Jasmine yanked out a big silvery sparkled dick, held it up, and said, "Nah, not this" and threw it back in the bag. Too bad, that one was a good one. Next she pulled out a blue string-of-pearls dildo that measured four inches long and had the pathetic circumference of a man's thumb. She said her new man paralleled this gem. I said, "Wow, his dick is shaped like a string of pearls?" She threw it at my head, laughed, and dug for another one, a small dick I used for sticking in brave men's behinds. "This one is his." It was small, but she said that love is the best aphrodisiac, not a big cock.

Most of my friends knew that I had quite a large collection of silicone dildos and other sex toys, choice instruments collected along the way. Size does matter, but bigger isn't necessarily always better. My desires are ever-changing and I get in all different kinds of moods when it comes to what is needed to fulfill me for a night. My collection of dildos ranges from four inches to a two-foot-long, double-ended dildo that I only ever use to hit people over the head with. I have a little something for everyone and I have a little too much for some. Not for Jasmine, though. She is always willing to try a new toy. This is best accomplished with several of her favorite alcoholic beverages, Adios Mother Fuckers, a disgustingly sweet blue Long Island iced tea that is sure to not only guarantee a person to give in but to also give up any inkling of class.

Jasmine had a history of breaking into my dildo collection and playing with my toys when I was not home. A few years back when we were still together I left her sleeping in bed while I went to a rehearsal for a play I was in. When I came home I found my favorite pink vibrator in pieces on the ground, kicked back under the bed like a tossed aside pair of panties. I was crestfallen to find that my rubber friend, wires exposed and batteries strewn, had suffered an untimely and painful death. I knew Jasmine was the culprit. She denied it until very recently when she asked me, "Whatever happened to that vibrating dildo I broke?" I wrestled her to the ground and flipped her over my knee, giving her a well-deserved spanking.

A good rule to follow about penis size is that guys with big dicks talk about it; guys with small dicks don't. I have only met one man who broke this rule and who bragged about his giant nine-and-half-inch member but when it came down to it, whipped out a pathetic and pruned three inches. I ran from the backseat of his car, never to return again. Some men will offer up the fact that their dick is not that big—but a lot more men won't say a word. Silence is golden when figuring out penis size.

Men also seem to be deaf when it comes to gossip about their penises. My friend Eve, one of the most quick-witted and funny people I know, always has something clever to say on the subject of men. She met a good-looking man on the patio of a popular bar in Los Angeles while we were out one spring night. He addressed her, she turned to speak to him for a few brief seconds, and then swiftly spun back around to look squarely at

Katie Moran

me, whispering, "He has a small dick." I cracked up. I tapped him on the shoulder to look him in the eyes and verify her assumptions. Indeed he did have a small one. Hours and many drinks later, Eve and I saw the same man exiting the bar. I drunkenly blurted out, "Hey, there's the guy with the small dick!" Our male friend silenced me, embarrassed.

Eve interjected, "Don't worry, he couldn't hear you. Men can never hear that they have a small dick."

A good way to find out is to ask another guy. At first they will be horror struck that you would ask but if the guy is truly your friend, he will 'fess up. My friend Talia wanted to date my brother's friend, Aaron. I suspected Aaron only had a thin five inches at most, and I asked my brother if he had ever seen it. For a few seconds my brother cringed at my question and turned his face away in disgust but after a moment his macho side took over and he admitted, "I saw it in the locker room after water polo practice one time and it had been in hot water for a while so I know it was not the pool's fault. We nicknamed him Mini Me. Don't tell anyone I told you or I'll kill you!" His honesty spared poor Talia another disappointing encounter.

My friend Hayley has an excellent way of discovering a potential boyfriend's penis size. She invites the man to an activity where either bathing suits or workout clothes are required; hiking is her favorite first date because the man will sweat and his clothes will cling to him, revealing the silhouette of his penis. If it is summertime, Hayley invites her mate to the beach or to her house for a dip in the hot tub. One time she purposely dumped a plate of chicken-cordon-bleu in her date's lap so that he had to actually take off his jeans and wrap himself in the thin white towel she provided.

Another time one of her plans backfired when she dated a gentleman by the name of Devin. She invited him to a barbecue at the tennis club where she belonged. They decided to take a swim but when he came out of the men's changing room in his white trunks, Hayley was not the only one in for a complete surprise. Every one of the club members gathered around the pool stared at his assets. His gigantic dick was so long that it hung out from the bottom of his trunks, nearly grazing his knee. Older women recoiled in horror as he bounced on the diving board, nearly knocking out small children with his swinging pendulum. As her date hit the water, attention shifted to a red-faced Hayley who had nowhere to run from this massive nightmare.

She did the only thing she could think of to save herself from further embarrassment when he emerged from the water, his trunks dripping and clinging to his giant snakelike penis. She waited by the edge of the pool with a towel and wrapped it around Devin's waist; then she led him to a pool supply room and gave him a hand job. She reported to me that it took both of her hands, a bottle of suntan oil, and her entire body leaning into it to finally get him off. When he did, his load shot across the room and hit a bottle of chlorine with an audible splat.

Around the same time as Hayley's incident with Devin I was dating a really great guy. He was charming and funny, a perfect gentleman, but strangely enough I have completely forgotten his name. The fact that he had a forgettable penis might have something to do with my lapse of memory. He and I had the best month of our lives together until it came time to sleep together.

We had met at a party being thrown in a house on the top of a mountain overlooking the ocean. It was a magical setting and I was enjoying his pleasant company and the fact that he was such a gentleman. The best thing about him was that he liked me and he told me that again and again. At this point, I was conditioned to fall for aloof men like Austin who acted as if they were doing me a favor sticking around. This guy was a welcome change. He and I spent many evenings at this party house on the hill, taking dips in the pool and then warming up

Katie Moran

in the hot tub, sipping Cristal. And no, he was not rich but my friend who threw the parties at his mom's pad was and he had no qualms about cracking open case after case of her bubbly and sharing it with all of his comrades.

One night in the pool my top had conveniently fallen off and we wound up inside the house, looking for a towel. The rest of my bathing suit was lost in a sexy and rhythmic make-out session with him. When it came time to take it to the next level, I reached under his trunks to feel for his cock. Hmm, not very big at all, I thought. I hoped it had to do with the cold water of the swimming pool but as I stroked it and stroked it some more, I realized with horror that it might not grow anymore. However, my date's face was growing with pleasure as I prayed that he had not reached full size. My hopes were shattered when he said, "Oh, my God, I have never been this hard. You are so hot and I can't believe how good this feels."

The only thing that came to mind at that moment was "Shit." I thought that the sheer lust and attraction I had for him would compensate for the lack of size but it did not. I could barely feel his middle-finger-sized penis. He and I split up the next day and he was crushed, as was I. I cried over the loss of such a great man. He kept begging and begging for an answer but I did not have the heart to tell him the real reason why. He said he wanted me to meet his mother and hoped that maybe she could talk to me about why we broke up. I thought to myself, "Well, if you happen to take after your father, I doubt I will have much explaining to do."

I dated this guy when I was fairly young and, although I intuitively knew he might have a size issue, I liked him so much that I ignored my gut feeling in the hopes that it was not true. Now that I am a little older, such discoveries are not as devastating as they once were. There are countless women walking around displaying their plastic surgery, and letting their fake breasts say what they can't express verbally—that is, "I feel less than beautiful. I feel inadequate. I want to look better and I want more people to like me. I want men to want me. Don't stare at my rack but DO!" If so many women feel the need to surgically enhance, why don't men? I doubt there are as many men running to Beverly Hills surgeons' offices shelling out thousands for penile implant surgery as there are women buying fake breasts. If a man can pass up a girl because her breasts are small, women can certainly ditch a guy because his dick is too small. Life is too short to be in a miserable sexual relationship.

Because so many men lie about size, the only way to find out, ladies, is by pulling that tape measure out and sizing it yourself. My friend Jen will argue me to the grave on the size point. Although she likes a large penis and says it helps, she says sometimes big is "too big" and it hurts, especially when the man doesn't know what he is doing and is carelessly throwing it around like a weight that has flown free from its pendulum. She is currently dating a thirty-seven-year-old man with a three-and-a-half-inch dick, whom she claims is her best lover yet. He is highly experienced in technique, and his penis fits in her in such a way that it hits her G spot every time they have sex and she has multiple orgasms—one every three minutes.

So, there is hope for the poorly endowed man. There is someone for everyone, a dick for every vagina or a dick for every dick. Maybe there is a woman born with an abnormally small vagina that will feel like she has struck gold when she meets the man of her dreams, who drops his pants for the first time and salutes her with three inches. I would still recommend that those men sharpen their oral sex skills, just in case.

My friend Sheryl loves girth and not length. If I have to hear, "Oh, my gaaawd, his big . . . thick . . . cock felt soooo good last night" one more time . . . but she does make a very good point. What is the use of a twelve-inch cock if all it does is poke at

Katie Moran

your cervix but barely grazes the vaginal walls? Every woman has to find out what is "fitting" for her. The most common request I hear from women is a man with a six-inch-long but fairly thick penis.

Penis size is a major conversation topic among women. My friend Robin has gone back to her deadbeat ex-husband time after time to experience more of some giant cock. She said that men with large dicks can get away with far more bad behavior such as cheating, physical and verbal abuse, laziness, and dependence on a woman for financial security, while men with small penises have to work much harder to sustain a relationship. It is a science of checks and balances. I can only compare it to a neck injury. When one part of the body is completely damaged and rendered weaker than usual, the rest of the body such as the back and the shoulders have to make up for the deficiency by working ten times harder. Men with small penises have to really thrive in areas such as romance, financial stability, and that thing called love.

My most famous theory about dick size is my car-radio theory. Talia called me from her mobile phone while on the road. She had been in New York for a month on business and was hoping to have some decent sex while she was there. Talia is a big fan of vacation sex, the kind of sex you can have with a stranger that lives so far away they can barely afford to call you let alone come visit you.

Talia had been in a stressful seminar all day and her attempts to find a one-night stand in the hotel lounge had ended in disaster. Her last chance for vacation sex would be during the next seven days, when she would be staying at her parents' ranch in Texas. "Oh good, a cowboy," I thought; cowboys should have big dicks, right? I wasn't sure. I have never slept with a real cowboy—only LA cowboys, the kind that model ripped up flannel shirts and faux vintage jeans for Hilfiger. Now that Talia was going out to the ranch she would be able to finally prove my theory that men with big dicks rarely care about their shoes or their cars. I was quite sure a man who was packing would wear the same pair of cowboy boots until their feet are nearly touching the pavement through the holes.

Every guy I have ever dated who had a big dick was also very careless with the appearance of his car. This does not apply to drug dealers, ballers, and other such misfits who make sure their Cadillac Escalades and GMC Yukons are fitted with the finest stolen stereo systems and chrome wheels that spin even when the car is sitting still. Personally, I've always thought these particular rims are a bad idea. Cops in Los Angeles are trigger happy as it is, why would we want to provoke them even more by appearing to be rolling through a stoplight when in fact our cars are at a dead stop? I especially would not want to draw attention to myself if I had a kilo of cocaine in my trunk and an arrest record that I had tattooed down my forearm for shits and giggles.

My mind was back on cowboys and penises as Talia shouted in the phone, "Horny horny horny me so horny horny horny!" Talia had a tendency to be rather irritating and childish when she had not gotten laid in too long. I always advise women who are seeking out a well-endowed man to take note of their appearance and their car. If there is a broken radio or any other really obvious damage, like a snapped off antenna or cracked windshield, the dick is at least an inch bigger than average, I have found out. Of course, there are those guys that have broken-down cars, cheap shoes, and still have small dicks. This is what we call a LOSER.

Austin had NO radio in his car at all, just a space with exposed wiring where the radio once lived, probably with a previous owner. I even dated a woman who had a cracked windshield on her brand new car and she turned out to the best female lover I have ever had. My car is in near perfect condition and my stereo system is very high quality. What does that say about me as a lover? Maybe I should take a hammer to my CD changer and see if I get more compliments in bed.

My friend Zeke and I go out regularly and hit all of the beach bars together. When he gets drunk he has the habit of talking about his "big" dick. Beautiful women often stop talking mid-sentence to turn around to listen to him describe his member. Other women freeze mid-slurp on their mojitos and turn to walk toward Zeke. Once he has gathered a crowd of drunken female onlookers, I break the sad news to the collection of women. Zeke's penis might be eight inches long but it is pencil thin. Zeke is like a brother to me, and he has sex every other night with his beautiful range of ladies so I do not feel bad if I dissuade a few from going to bed with him. Plus, when he is drunk he tends to not use protection and has called me frantic on more than one occasion with a grotesque, yet hilarious crabs or herpes scare. I think the late-night clinic in Malibu knows him by name now.

For those of you size queens out there, here is my method of determining penis size without having to see a man's car or assess his wardrobe. First of all, there is just plain common sense. A man who has small, shifty eyes and a nervous demeanor should be avoided at all costs. Men who cannot look directly at you are hiding something. Dick-size insecurity and poor sexual performance is really evident just by looking at someone. A man with a large dick is most likely confident, still, and usually has a wry smile that says teasingly, "I know something that you don't know." It took me a while to get to the point in my life where I was attracted to men that exude confidence. The first guy I was with was so insecure and damaged, although I had no clue until years later that he was so mentally askew. In general, I have found that it is more beneficial to surround myself with people who are confident and self-assured than people, whether friends or boyfriends, who are constantly seeking the approval of others.

Sheryl and I play the "Guess the Penis" game all the time. We see a man and estimate his size. Then, if one of us is interested in him, we report to the other if our speculations were correct. One guy, Chuck LaBall, had hit on my two best friends and me. He had that look of a guy with a teeny tiny dick; squinty eyed and self-conscious. Mia screamed, "Eeew, get him AWAY from me. He has LITTLE DICK EYES!" We kept ignoring him and turning him down but he would still hit on us individually on different occasions, as if we had never met him before. I can only deduce that he had hit on so many women and been shut down so many times that he truly could not discern one face from the next. Another friend of ours named Iris did not heed our warning and slept with him anyway. She confirmed our presuppositions. She said it was so small that he might as well have stuck it in her belly button because there was no friction going on anywhere else.

I had my own run-in with a case of a penis junior. When I met Brookfield, I should have known. No, no, I take that back. I totally knew, but just ignored my dick-dar (penis radar) altogether. Brookfield was a perfectly groomed trust-fund baby whom I had met in an upscale trendy hotel bar on Sunset Boulevard. His eyes were small and insecure, hiding behind expensive wire-framed glasses, and he had a slight under bite and a forced laugh; but, he was rich and very smart. In LA it is hard to find an educated man who can hold a conversation beyond talking about himself and mentioning, "I just auditioned for this pilot today and I am hoping for a callback." I lost myself in his travel stories and arguments over the latest philosophical reading. He also smelled really good. He was interesting, and strange. I looked down past his crisp white Oxford and into the lap of his Brooks Brothers slacks. Hmmm. No bulge.

He saw me look and began to stutter. This was a very bad sign. When a man cannot control his speech when the subject of his penis is brought to the forefront, run to the hills, girls. I

Katie Moran

made the mistake of sleeping with him against my better judgment. It was bad. Not only was it small (well under five inches), the bastard could not even keep it hard for more than a minute. He said I made him nervous. I stayed with him for three months thinking that I could help him with his problem. How nervous could he have been with me after the thirtieth time we tried to have sex? He needed to see a doctor or perhaps just take a trip to a bathhouse and explore what in retrospect seems like his latent homosexuality.

After we broke up, I went to a party and had a few too many cocktails and brought my best friend over to his house at 4 AM for a little last-ditch effort to let him express his manhood. After all, I didn't dislike the guy. He was respectful, charming, and fun to be around. But, that is not enough reason to stay in a relationship with him. I am a size queen—I like them big and hard. Or, as Bobby says, "Real big and real hard." I also like my men to be smooth, skilled, and hard until I have had as many orgasms as possible. When we knocked on his door, Brookfield was happy to see me. He was groggy but did not appear as timid as he usually did when we were together.

So, my last little favor for him was a three-way with my friend and me. He started off great. He got right into the action and was making out with us both, kissing us passionately and massaging our backs. He knew just what to do in the act of foreplay. But once the fooling around turned to intercourse (my friend was the unlucky one and she volunteered to go first), the poor little prep-schooler could not even keep his wood with two beautiful women fondling each other right in front of him. She looked at me and held out her forefinger, bending it like a limp dick and smashing it into the palm of her hand like a crumpled piece of cardboard. Performance anxiety? We were not going to stick around to find out. We went home and had some gratuitous sex with each other.

Brookfield and I had a friendly lunch a year later. He had a hard-on the whole entire time and he still looked at me with those little-dick eyes. When I said the word "Viagra" and his face turned red, the question in my mind was quickly answered. Good for him, I thought. At least he was trying something to improve his condition. Whatever works. But, not for me. I like the real thing and so do my girlfriends. A little training in the study of human behavior can be a big payoff in the bedroom.

Katie Moran

10

Acting Out

My most rebellious activities always seem to occur when I'm in a fight with a significant other. Is it wrong to harness anger into some sort of activity or is it better to sit in the feeling, wallow in it, and possibly work through it? People express their discomfort and pain in a variety of ways. Many times these avenues of expression are self-destructive or harmful to the overall outcome of a relationship. Dealing with problems in a constructive way is something that is established by years of practice. In the meantime, we can witness all sorts of outrageous conduct from others and from ourselves. There are many different types of behavior associated with acting out.

After plowing through relationships at lightning speed, I realized that sometimes there is an option other than breaking

up. I had been with my boyfriend Carlo for about a year and had grown used to the fact that we never had a fight or even a small disagreement, other than my complaints about his cat, Stacie. Stacie was a horrible animal. She hated me, once even spitting in my face when I was sleeping. She was like a dirty trucker spitting out tobacco on the side of the road. She was the most worthless creature I have ever encountered but Carlo loved her so I had to put up with her. Carlo even went so far as to insist that I pretend to like Stacie, for his sake.

That was the most difficult part. I am a terribly honest person and I found it painful to pet Stacie's greasy fur as she stiffened and hissed at me. Another time I woke up in agony and found the jealous little shit's teeth clamped down on my hand. I sometimes prayed there would be a terrible fire and Carlo and I would flee the apartment to safety while poor Stacie, aka "Satan," was lost in the blaze. It was just a little fantasy I had.

Other than that, Carlo and I seemed like the perfect couple. We had fallen in love in such an easy way—the first time I saw him I knew I wanted to be his girlfriend. The best part about our courtship was that I always knew how he felt about me too. There were no games and no misunderstandings; all of our friends assumed that we would eventually get married. We bought a house together and had plans to move in; that was when it all came crashing down. The only way to describe the way it felt when our relationship turned to shit was like being in some weird dream. Imagine yourself standing in the middle of a gorgeous Italian square enjoying the scenery and all of a sudden something flies up your ass. It was just as much of a shock to me and right away I knew that I was the one who was going to suffer.

Carlo had been feeling pressure in his own life and did not know how to express it. His form of acting out was to drink . . . excessively. When we met I told him that I would never date an alcoholic; I had worked hard to harness my party-girl reputation and I wanted a mate who had done the same. Hearing this, Carlo decided to be a closet drinker rather than tell me he had a problem. I first saw a glimpse of trouble when we decided to go to San Francisco together. I arrived at the airport at 3 and went to the check-in counter where we had agreed to meet. By 5, he still wasn't at the airport, and his work was calling me looking for him. He had never shown up at the office and hadn't called in sick. I thought the worst, of course. He had either had a heart attack or his bitch cat had mauled him to death.

When he finally surfaced, one hour before our flight, he said he had taken two Xanax and drunk a bottle of tequila. Looking back I realize that the pressure of going on a trip with a new girlfriend and trying to finish up a pile of work had triggered his outburst but at the time I was utterly confused. I was so in love with Carlo that I forgave him immediately but he ended up repeating this behavior countless times. On our one-year anniversary he was so drunk that he drove two hours in the wrong direction on our way to Santa Barbara before I realized he was trashed and took the wheel.

I was a very naïve girl at this time and even though Carlo is a bad liar, I accepted most of what he told me. I wanted to believe the best possible explanations when in actuality, I should have been expecting the worst. There were countless nights that I made him dinner or went out of my way for him and he would not show up because he would be passed out drunk in his bed. When I would talk with him about it, all I was given was yelling and screaming, and he often found a way to blame me. I kept taking him back and taking him back, as he was making feeble attempts to get sober and go to AA meetings. I say "feeble" attempts because Carlo would never admit the one thing that is required to get help for a drinking problem: that he

Katie Moran

was an alcoholic. He thought he was better than "those" people and as a result he is still a problem drinker to this day.

Carlo's acting out by drinking drove us out of our plans to live together; drove him out of a six-figure income and any semblance of hygiene; and drove me out of the passion I had previously felt for him. The magic had died when he took that first drink some random weekday at ten in the morning. As much as I wanted things to work out between us, I knew that there would be no future.

Carlo was an absolute angel about 95 percent of the time. The other 5 percent, he was living hell. He left me in San Diego once for two days, opting to drink three bottles of cheap Rite-Aid vodka rather than drive down to pick me up. He nearly lost a second job but luckily I covered for him, saying he was suffering from food poisoning. I was so sick of cleaning up after him, worrying about him, and not trusting him. It happened so many times in a six-month period that I lost count. We stayed together and he cleaned up his act so that he was only having about one bad day of drinking a month. This was usually on an important day like when my mom was coming over to have lunch with us. My mom really loved him but also knew that I could not go on any longer in this stagnant existence.

I had no idea the toll that Carlo's acting out was taking on me. He was able to drink to relieve his incredible stress, the pressures of his business, and the constant disasters with the new house that he had to deal with on his own because he had scared me out of our living plans. I had no outlet. I was no longer a heavy drinker or avid partygoer and had given up a lot of my old friends to dedicate most of my time to the relationship with Carlo. This was a huge mistake, because perhaps if I had maintained some of those friendships I would have had more of a balance in my life.

One particular night when Carlo and I had called it quits again (we broke up at least ten times in an eight-month period), I answered the phone and it was Jasmine. She was crying because her crazy boyfriend had hit her again. I told her to come over so we could talk about how messed up our love lives were. Instead, we ended up drinking a bottle of wine and nearly sleeping together. I suppose it would not have been considered cheating since Carlo and I were broken up, but I knew in the back of my mind that it was not really over. Even though I could not go through with it, the feeling of temptation was enough of an escape for me. Temptation became my vice and my method of acting out.

I never have to look for temptation; it has a habit of finding me wherever I am. Temptation is both a form of acting out and a destructive outlet when everything is going just fine. The worse the communication between me and Austin became, the more I seemed to be confronted by temptation. I was tempted by everything from cigarettes to sex and from moving across country to becoming a stripper. Falling victim to temptation is a cry for help, a sign to oneself that things are not acceptable. At the beginning of my relationship with Carlo, everything was so perfect that it seemed magical and unbelievable. The sex was amazing with him, sometimes lasting all night long. I never dreamed of looking at another person. Beautiful people could have crossed my face every five minutes, and they probably did, but my eyes were not open to see anyone except him.

One of the first indications that our relationship had fallen from its pedestal was when I was out driving one morning. I had my eyes on a sexy young guy on a mountain bike who had craned his neck to look back at me. I was so busy smiling at him and dreaming about inviting him into my car for a little roadside rumble that I hardly noticed the approaching curb and mailbox. Though I hit the curb I missed the mailbox; Carlo was the furthest thing from my mind.

There is a difference between temptation and transgression. The problem that haunts a lot of former Catholic-school girls like me is that gnawing feeling that we are always doing something wrong. Growing up Catholic, coupled with growing up in a cauldron of Italian guilt, made for an upbringing full of self-questioning and shame. I escaped from the guilt by partying and drinking away my conscience. I also escaped the feeling by confronting the problem head on. I would do the exact thing that was deemed bad or wrong. I would wear the offensive clothes, I would make out with the "bad" guys, and I would be seen in the wrong places. Many of my fellow schoolgirls did the same, finding solace in escapism, while others kept up the moralities inflicted upon them throughout their schooling.

These girls still think that having pre-marital sex is wrong (even though they have had plenty of it). These are the girls that whisper when they talk about sex, and these are the same girls whose faces crinkle in disgust at the thought of having sex with another woman, more than one person at a time, or not being married by the age of twenty-six. My best friend passed on her dream of an outdoor wedding to be married in church; the same church that we had chewed gum in, cursed in, and dreaded the day we would ever have to return to it for Christmas services with our aging mothers. These girls had become what we all grew up hating. Their idea of acting out was to do Christmas shopping in December instead of in October or having sex with their husbands on just-washed sheets before eating a sit-down dinner.

I would love to say that I found all of my satisfaction in life from doing things that I felt I had permission to do, like showing up to work on time or dating the "perfect" mate. I would love to enjoy all the things that I am "allowed" to do or allow myself to enjoy the things I do anyway without thinking there is something wrong or abnormal with them. Some examples of the activities that I enjoy but often question myself for doing include: drinking a beer at four in the morning alone while writing; having a relationship with a woman; humanizing my dog;

and taking drives to nowhere. I wish I could accept myself for all the things that other people, and sometimes myself, often raise their eyebrows about. Every day I am one step closer to actualizing this goal.

In the meantime, I find gratification in stepping outside of the box, as Oprah advises us to do. Of course, I am not sure if what she means by this includes kicking the entire box aside and mothering a child with a lesbian while teaching Pilates and/or transcendental sex to sailors, one of which is the sperm donor of the lesbian's baby OR if she means just taking a different hiking route than the one you are used to.

Maybe it means something different to each and every one of us. Maybe I can step outside my box by NOT having that threesome while others can switch it up by just knitting a different color sweater that day. Maybe transgression for me is what is ordinary for "normal" people. I do have to admit that having a beef sandwich at a high school football game seems almost pornographic to me while watching real porn being filmed live is just old hat. I have become jaded by many people's standards. Sometimes we just have to make our own definitions for things that are not fitting for us.

A lot of my friends wondered why I did not just break up with Carlo. A lot of it had to do with the depression he felt when he drank. I feared that he would fall deeper into ruin and that by breaking up with him I would somehow be responsible for this. Carlo would guilt me into staying with him, saying that everyone in his life had walked out on him and that being in a relationship meant staying around even for the difficult moments. He made some very good points but at the end of the day the reason why I stayed with Carlo was love. He was handsome, an extremely gifted musician and painter, and highly intelligent. We had something truly special that I had never encountered and feared I would never find again. We were the elusive soul mates.

Katie Moran

I loved him very much and deep down I wanted things to work out between us. Mainly though I just wanted him to not have a drinking problem. But my mom reminded me that you could wish in one hand and shit in the other, and which one filled up first? My mom has a blunt viewpoint on relationships. She thinks she killed her first husband by simply wishing him away. Her second husband, my stepfather, is also a heavy drinker. His idea of acting out however is eating a gallon of Dreyer's Grand at two in the morning.

My relationship with Carlo had too many moments that were tiresome and painful; at the end of the day though I loved Carlo and the good times we had together when he was sober made it hard to leave. There were a few other problems in our relationship when it came to the day-to-day stuff, yet nothing out of the ordinary. But every time he drank, I felt like he was cheating on me. It was as if alcohol was his other girlfriend and he was choosing her over me. When he drank he would literally disappear and not call me for days. I would repeatedly take him back and eventually it reached the point that I would not even get angry with him anymore. I wanted all of those magical feelings to reappear and so I stayed with Carlo against my better judgment. I stayed in the relationship until all that was left was love.

I spent many weekends at Carlo's house and one Sunday I invited my mom to come over for lunch. Carlo had an extensive work project to complete so he said he would not be available to eat lunch with us but that he would come out of his home office to say hi to my mom, who loved him. When we woke up he made a big Greek salad for my mom and then went into his office and shut the door. My mother and I ended up spending more time together than I had originally planned for and when we got back from five hours of shopping we found Carlo passed out in bed. My brother had been there and he told me later that Carlo had finished a couple of bottles of vodka. It was really bad timing, yet I loved him so much that once again I forgave him for it. He apologized and said that the stress of having a job he hated was too much for him. I was angry and irritated at Carlo, yet I didn't tackle these feelings; instead, I buried the discomfort deep inside.

The week after this incident I went out several times; I danced with several women at the only good lesbian bar in West Hollywood, the place where all the hot girls who like girls hang out. I danced good and close to all of them and even took some straight guys along for the ride. I was not looking to meet anyone, but a young boy caught my eye. I was feeling good from my raspberry vodkas and I returned this boy's gaze more than once. For a moment I wondered what a straight guy was doing in a lesbian bar but then I quickly came to my senses.

Tons of straight guys flocked to this bar to see hot women making out with each other or hoping to jump in and take part in some action themselves. I wondered if this cute boy was even able to drink; he looked about high school age. He finally approached me and I couldn't resist flirting with him. His name was Nate and he was a professional surfer. He was gorgeous and a bit older than I had expected—he was twenty and still in college. He lived at home with his mom and went snowboarding every weekend in the winter.

I was fairly sloshed so I cannot be absolutely positive but I think I slipped up. I might even have kissed him. I know I gave him my number because he called me two days later. My two girl friends who were with me that night were impressed by my ability to meet someone after not dating for so long. I was shocked myself. They had had no luck that evening and ended up going home and screwing each other. They were both straight but with enough liquor almost anyone can be convinced, and they were intoxicated. They tried to convince me to come with them but the guilt of being in a relationship and risking hurting Carlo was too much pressure for me. Every time

Carlo looked at me and told me how perfect I was, I could never have lived with myself if I had gone to bed with not only one but two women. Plus, I knew both of them would have turned out to be lousy lays. And nothing compounds the guilt of cheating on your boyfriend or girlfriend more than being punished by terrible sex.

Nate and I talked on the phone and I was honest with him about Carlo. He said he had been dating a woman that lived on the East Coast but it was not going anywhere. Although Carlo and I were heading for a break-up, I knew that cheating on him was wrong so I just enjoyed the thrill of being very, very tempted. Nate and I went out for coffee one night and talked for about two hours. Nothing happened. I secretly hoped that Carlo would slip again and that I could break up with him for good this time. I was sick of giving him chance after chance with no resolve and no improvement. I was ready to leave and never come back. Well, I got what I wished for, and it was bittersweet. Carlo drank for three days straight and missed a very important wedding we were supposed to go to together. I broke up with him and he barely remembered even having an argument the next day. But I felt entirely free from the burden of that sinking ship of a relationship.

I had freedom that I had not felt in two years. It was not just the freedom of being single; it was the freedom of not having to worry about another person's fuck-ups. And when we finally did go out, Nate and I had a fabulous time on our date. Twenty-year-olds have the ability of lifting a massive amount of weight from the mind. At least this one did. He was so innocent and sweet; all he wanted to do was to have fun, the innocent type of fun. We watched videos and ate pizza on the floor. It was like being in high school again. It was quite a contrast to steam cleaning a carpet after a thirty-four-year-old drunk has spilled Coca Cola and hot sauce all over it (he never spilled a drop of that vodka, though).

The first night Nate came over to my house I forced Jasmine to stick around because I was scared of being alone with someone new. After all, I had not dated in almost two years. Every time Jasmine left the room Nate and I kissed. He rubbed my leg and held my hand. It was so exciting because it was new, yet something was missing. Nate did not know all the weird nicknames I had for things, and he did not know what made me laugh. He also did not know how I liked a guy to smell. I was incredibly turned on; I lost my breath just sitting next to Nate. He really liked me, and I liked him but I could not be with him in the capacity that was fair to him. He wanted a girlfriend and I just wanted someone to take my mind off Carlo.

Nothing happened between Nate and me that night, and as soon as Nate left my house Carlo called. He was so sweet and as we talked I realized how much I missed him. I missed the familiarity. Breaking up with someone you love is so hard; it is easier to hate the person. But I did not hate Carlo, I loved him. He was the greatest person except for the part of him that drank at all the wrong times. One would think that going back to my life with Carlo would not even be an option once Nate entered the picture. I should have jumped at the chance to be with someone young, handsome, and exciting. But this time the thought of a new lover was not thrilling; it was unknown and uncomfortable.

Carlo wanted me back and was ready to do anything, or so he said. He didn't blame me for breaking up with him and he knew I had to look out for myself. Through unbearable tears he said all the right things; he was breaking my heart as I was breaking his. But Carlo's acting out had triggered mine. I would never have given any guy my number if I were not rebelling against my disgust at Carlo. I did not want to give my freedom up. I felt I had earned it and I did not want to go back to a stifling existence with my boyfriend. I wanted the best of both worlds, which was impossible in this situation.

Katie Moran

I let my bout with acting out run its course before getting back together with Carlo. I knew we would have to work twice as hard at our relationship but the thing we had was so rare and precious that I felt he was worth it. The first night that I had him back in bed with me, his black eye from hitting himself in the face while uncorking a wine bottle nearly healed, was better than any affair could have been. We did not have sex that night, but just lying next to him with my arm draped across his body felt better than making out with a hot twenty-year-old. Oh God! What was I thinking? I must be crazy. Love tends to have that effect on people.

There are tons of other ways to act out in a relationship. It does not always have to involve things that are so seriously damaging to a relationship that they would prevent reunification. In Los Angeles, two of the most popular choices are exercise and food. Exercise being the healthier choice, of course, and food being many people's comforting downfall. After a fight with a lover, your favorite thing to do might be to avoid his or her phone calls for a few days, go out on the town and tie one on, or have people report back to your mate that you are doing "Great!" without him.

Perhaps you enjoy making your man jealous by calling up an ex and having lunch in a restaurant where you know you will be seen, maybe even by a waiter who is your boyfriend's best friend. Some women act out by eating too much food, as I said, or committing even more self-destructive acts. Others burden their girl friends with the boring details of their temporary separation. I know one woman who stole all her boyfriend's credit cards and took a trip to Vegas after they had a bad argument. Although women act out in these relatively harmless ways, many women also choose to just plain cheat. It is more prevalent than I had ever imagined.

Some friends that I have known for years and have had possibly a thousand conversations with only came out and admitted to cheating on their husbands and boyfriends when they knew I was writing a book and thought that I might have some answers. I do not endorse cheating but I recognize its frequency. I know that we are all human and some things are unavoidable. People make mistakes and that is just life. Self-control is a skill that not all of us possess in a large capacity.

My friend Jordan has been on and off with her boyfriend, John, for nearly fifteen years and she is an avid and experienced cheater—but only when she and John are not speaking. One time John went out of town with a female friend (oh, sure, those go over about as well as lipstick in Catholic school) and never even called Jordan to say good-bye. She had started a new job and didn't even get a call from John to wish her good luck. Jordan did something she had not done in years. She called a number out of the back of the LA Weekly. She arrived at her favorite restaurant on Santa Monica Boulevard and was met by a familiar face, Andre, the maître d'. He gave her a wink and remarked that he had not seen her for a while.

She slid casually into the seat at her favorite table and awaited her guest; a very young man dressed in a crisp, pale blue shirt and creased slacks. She wasted no time in sliding the young man $200 under a white cloth napkin and summoning him into the women's restroom. She ordered him to lift up her skirt and take her from the back. After fifteen minutes she yelled at him for not following her instructions; he was supposed to be wearing a white Oxford and not a blue. He finished up and followed her back to the table. He started to sit back down when she shooed him away and insisted upon eating her dinner alone. The young man tried to make conversation, exchange a phone number, get a name but Jordan would have none of it. He was just another hooker to her. He was dismissed like all of the rest of them, a victim of her damaged heart.

One Friday night, an old friend Greg, a twenty-seven-year-old water polo player with a perfectly cut abdomen, big blue

Katie Moran

eyes, and a bulge, approached Jordan in his Speedos. The game was on for Jordan. As if the male prostitute was not enough of a crime, Jordan wanted to have a bit of free sex with Greg.

She made a date with Greg and told him to expect to come back to her place. Right before the date, John called. Jordan let it go to voice mail; she did not want to talk to him and let him change her mind about her plans for the evening. He said he loved her and missed her—she hit erase on her voice mail. She was still too angry to talk to John. Jordan had a great evening of sex and debauchery with Greg, thinking about John in the back of her mind while Greg was inside of her. The next day she called John back and they got together again. She said she felt the need to act out in order to stop feeling so angry and hurt by John.

I was not surprised to find out that Jordan and John had broken up for good months later. Jordan is now married to a man fifteen years her junior. He has a drug problem but the sex is amazing and she has remained faithful to him throughout the hardships they have sustained. I believe that any man who can keep Jordan out of other men's pants is the man for her. Oh, and she loves him too.

Acting out by cheating may lessen the hurt but it will never completely erase it. For Jordan, cheating helped her feel that she had evened the score in her own way. Hey, whatever works. I am not an avid fan of cheating; I guess because I always hear my mother's voice saying, "Do unto others as you would have done to you." I would not want my boyfriend or girlfriend to cheat on me, and I would not want to even suspect that they would. Trust is so important in a relationship that once it is gone, it is nearly impossible to completely get back. If the relationship gets to that point, I usually call it quits before screwing someone else.

One Tuesday night while I was still dating Jasmine, she was in one of her drunken blackouts and admitted to me that she had met some girl online and was going to a party with her that weekend. I was irate but the next day Jasmine clearly did not remember telling me because she lied and said she was going to the party with her friends. I did not talk to her for four days, and I acted out by calling this woman from my past and setting up a date to go to the beach with her. My intent was not to sleep with her, just kind of get my mind off of Jasmine and her Internet ho. All I ended up getting was a bacterial infection from the polluted Pacific Ocean.

I was so enraged the whole day at the beach and the entire night of the alleged party that I could not get Jasmine off my mind. I called her and she did not call me back. I even showed up with my friend Mia at the bar where the party was to see if I could catch her in the act. The act of what, I don't know; I just wanted to let her know that I was on top of her. It was probably my fear of being rejected, or of being played for a fool, that had driven me. She wasn't there. Then I really felt like a fool, and it was my own doing. I had become psychotic. "This isn't me!" I remember thinking. But I still did not want to be home alone with my thoughts after she hadn't called me all weekend. In my vindictive state, I went out by myself on the Sunday night following the party and met about four different guys and gave them all my number.

When I did finally talk to Jasmine I found out that one of her best friends had died over the weekend so she was not able to do anything at all. That would explain why I didn't see her at the bar that night. Now I was stuck with the wreckage of my acting-out fit. I had all these guys calling me and wasting my time, wanting to take me out, talk or have coffee. I didn't want anyone but Jasmine, but by this point I had made my life even more difficult because I was stuck trying to politely brush off all these other people. One of the guys turned out to be a phone stalker and called me thirty times a day without leaving a message. Thank God for caller ID. I had created this drama for nothing. Creating unnecessary drama is something my friends do all the time. They create a storyline for something that hasn't even taken place yet, or may never take place at all. I try to live in the present now and not speculate on what could happen or what my partner might have been doing when he or she wasn't with me. Speculation is tiresome and useless and I just wind up unhappy. I have now taken to more healthy ways of acting out when I am angry with a significant other—I exercise. Or, I go to the park with the dog and pretend to exercise. I do not even make fun of yoga anymore. In fact I tried it and I actually liked it. Or, I take my Jet Ski out on the lake and ride my troubles away. Sometimes the ocean is a great place to cleanse the soul too. Sitting on the beach and listening to the waves crash down erases much of my anger. Another great thing I like to do when I am upset is help another person out. I go to my mom's and clean her kitchen for her or help my brother with his high school English papers. Many of my friends find solace in retail therapy. They shop their pain away. They get exercise by walking around the mall for hours and even wind up with some great new looks. I cook. I make sure to choose a recipe that is really time-consuming and complicated so that it keeps my mind and hands occupied for hours. And I run. Because it is much better being active than cheating and winding up with a nasty itch from an STD. How would you explain *that* to a significant other?

11

Boundaries

I did not understand the full meaning of the word "boundary" until I was in a relationship. It is a line of demarcation, a mental and emotional fence. Boundaries are created to keep our sanity and maintain safety and peace for oneself. There are so many different types of boundaries in a relationship that it would take a year to list them all. Some examples are: No cheating, no using my credit card, no going into the kitchen when I'm cooking, and "Hey, sex with my friends is only allowed when I am there to watch!" Joking aside, all relationships need boundaries, and recognizing this and having enough courage to communicate about it with your partner is vital.

One agreement I had with Carlo after we had been dating for five months was that I was not to insult his family anymore. This was hard to do: They were horrible. His mother was a raging drunk and his brother a cross-dressing shoplifter. He had one sister that was saddled with three children whom she had turned into co-dependent morons. His sister's husband was a steroid-pumping bonehead who liked to shoot potato guns in the backyard. The oldest of the children was twelve at that time and could not even apply sunscreen to himself. The littlest one was still sucking her thumb at six and the nine-year-old boy still took daily naps with mommy. Carlo was over there all the time, buying them gifts and even food, since they always claimed they were broke. I found this hard to believe since she and her husband were both driving fifty-thousand-dollar cars.

I estimated that Carlo spent about five thousand a year on his sister's family. But when his birthday rolled around, his deadbeat ditz of a sister was too selfish to mail out a measly card. I could not believe I was dating into a family with so many creeps. My family is messed up, but at least they are generous and loving. These people were outrageous in the demands they made on their one upstanding relative, Carlo. No wonder he drank; I would too if my dad was a preacher and my sister was a twat.

I had a difficult time showing up at family functions with him and not cracking a smile when his brother Reynaldo/Janette would come out wearing a Donna Karan dress stolen from the local Bloomie's. I teased him incessantly about his insane family. I insulted them and tried to convince him to concentrate more on his own life than theirs. I razzed him to the point where one day he snapped. Carlo made a boundary with me to not insult his family, at least not to him. That's why I write. Someone other than me has to know how awful a 6'3" Brazilian man looks in a plum-colored A-line dress with matching shoes.

The boundary I set with Carlo was difficult to implement. At the beginning of our relationship, there were not many faults I could find with him. He was close to perfect and so was our relationship. But there was one thing that came up and it could not be ignored. One morning, via e-mail, he informed me that he was awake for an hour in the middle of the night, fondling me, and I never woke up. I was horrified. Not just that someone was touching me for an hour and I didn't wake up, but that he would want to do that to me while I was unconscious. I was irate and he did not understand why.

We argued about this for a long time; I explained that it made me uncomfortable to have someone touch me in a sexual manner without my permission. He could not understand what my problem was. He felt if we were in a relationship then I had already given my permission. I did not agree. I thought it was okay for him to touch me in a loving way but when his intention was to stimulate himself, I believed he needed to ask me first.

Carlo was very stubborn on this issue. He did not want to be constrained and wanted the freedom to touch me whenever he pleased. I could not believe it. Even after I told him that non-consensual sex of any kind makes me uncomfortable, he still pushed the issue and was actually mad at me, as if I had stolen something from him. He told me that he upheld the boundary that I had asked him to, although I would never know since I am a sound sleeper. Just in case, I wore a pair of boxer shorts to bed every night for about a month. At least that limited Carlo's access.

When I told my mother about this she was horrified—at me! She told me that I was a cold fish and that just by sleeping in bed naked with someone I was in a relationship with meant giving him or her full carte blanche to do whatever he or she wanted to my body at any time. She said, "You should be so lucky that you have someone who can't keep their hands off you. What I wouldn't give for your father to even sleep in the same bed with me . . ." and the rant went on and on. This is the same woman who, when asked how to keep a man, will reply, "Make them think you give a shit and swallow." She is a charming woman.

I have had to set plenty of boundaries with her as a parent as well. Now she is very respectful of my relationships with both men and women but she will still take the occasional stab at me and ask bitterly, "Do you think you could stay out of the gay bars for a month or two?" She would love for me to be completely straight. Yet she is the same person who embraces my girlfriends and is sometimes sadder than I am when we break up. She and I have much in common, as her second husband is also an alcoholic; Mom told me once, "Beer is his bitch." My step-father couldn't give up drinking for anything, not even his family. Finally Mom left him and moved into a new condo. She drew a boundary around her new home and kicked my step-dad out of her life. They are separated; it is still up in the air if they will draw the ultimate line between them and get the big "D" . . . divorce.

I don't know why I have the sleep-touching boundary but I do. I also don't like to be filmed or photographed without any clothes on, even if it is by someone I am in a relationship with. It just freaks me out. There are a few photos of me having sex floating around but I always make sure my head is not in the photo. Unless someone recognizes me by the way my pussy hair is shaved, I don't think I will have a problem. We all have boundaries that are customary to us and to our individual relationships. The important thing is to stick to our gut feelings about things and make sure our partners respect those wishes. Oh, and abide by theirs too.

After that, I kept my opinions about Carlo's family to myself. To prove it, I bought Carlo's brother a Christmas gift certificate to Victoria's Secret so he wouldn't have to steal thongs that year.

There are many boundaries in relationships when it comes down to sex. Carlo had one boundary for me when it came to having sex with women—I was not allowed to. I was used to guys who considered girls sleeping with other girls a treat and encouraged and applauded my escapades with other women. Carlo considered it cheating. He knew that I couldn't just have sex with a woman and toss her aside. He knew she would stick around and be added to my best friend roster, so I gave up any same-sex activity while in a relationship with Carlo. In retrospect, it was a good idea. It strengthened the bond the two of us had and forced me to be more creative in the ways he and I connected sexually. I don't know what I'll do if my next boyfriend gives me the thumbs up to have my cake and eat all of LA too. Maybe I will want to, maybe I won't. I guess I will know when I get there.

My friend Michelle and I are getting excited about the upcoming New Year. We have decided that it will bring an ISR, an Inner Sexual Revolution, for the both of us. We have promised each other that we will really go for it and knock down any boundaries that have been brewing inside of us. This means we will not be so self-conscious about our appearances or let our unimportant physical attributes infringe upon pleasure. This means that I will not let the fact that I hate how pale I have become force me to only have sex in minimal light. For Michelle, it means that that she won't let her self-consciousness of her less-than-washboard stomach prevent her from having an orgasm. Everyone has their own negative boundaries that they hold onto. Some men have problems with women touching or getting anywhere near their asses. They think it is "faggoty." Some men will not perform oral sex on women. I've said it before and I'll say it again: If you meet one of these men turn around and run! The worst ones are the men who expect a blowjob but would never return the favor to their partner. This kind of selfishness will be an indication of how they will act in all other aspects of the relationship.

Many homosexual men have set boundaries and rules for

Katie Moran

themselves. That is where the terms "top" and "bottom" came from. Bobby considers himself a "bottom" and I tease him about it all the time. I tell him, "You are a big old bottom, Bobby, maybe if you switched it up a bit you would get more respect out of your man." But Bobby prefers being a receiver to being a giver. Another friend of mine is a top and he browses the Internet looking for bottoms, a place to park his penis for a night. I asked him, "What do you do for them, what do they get out of it?" His response, "A blow job . . . or they can jerk off while I have sex with them." It seemed like a raw deal to me but this is a common dynamic. Some gay men do go both ways and prefer an equally versatile partner.

Many lesbians, especially butch lesbians, have strict boundaries in the bedroom. Some really take on the identity of "the man" and will not even let their lovers hold them. These same women refuse to consider any sort of penetration whether it is a finger or a dildo. To me, that seems like such a limiting lifestyle. True trust in relationships should be able to shatter these hang-ups. Who knows, a dyke might be surprised to find she actually enjoys being laid by a gorgeous feminine girl with a big purple strap-on. She may even like being "spooned" afterward.

There are boundaries found in both genders and in all sexual preferences. Claire, a friend of Carlo's, was the kind of girl who would dress as a naughty nurse on Halloween. However, she was dead-set against having anal sex with her boyfriend Tan, a goofy MIT guy. He constantly pushed the issue until she threatened to break up with him if he did not stop bringing it up. She explained to him that she had tried it but she didn't like it. He said, as I am sure we have all heard before, "But you haven't tried it with me." This was true and as a compromise she told him that he could go for the butt on their wedding night. Well, it worked; soon after that conversation she had a marriage proposal from Tan; and she planned to keep her word on the anal extravaganza.

A few months before the wedding, Tan drank too much and accidentally slipped into Claire's ass. She forcibly kicked him in the balls, knocking him to the floor. I thought she overreacted to this mistake. The sphincter-sex issue had taken on too much importance in their relationship. I encouraged her to forgive him because it really did seem like an accident. The two holes are so close together that you cannot expect someone to have perfect aim each and every time. Claire and Tan never did get married. It was not because Tan had slipped it into Claire's ass; it was because Claire was a tight-assed bitch.

There are boundaries when it comes to time limits in relationships. There is "me" time, "we" time, and sometimes no time for anything. I remember when Zeke was heading for trouble in the time department. Zeke is the kind of guy who needs time to go to the gym in the morning, time alone to read the paper and sit on the toilet, and time alone to work on his film projects. When he met his girlfriend Maeve and fell head over heels for her, I could see him about to crash and burn like a college student studying for finals. He was up all night having sex with her, skipping his breakfast and morning workout routines. He would cancel meetings with clients to bring her dry-cleaning over and feed her dog when she was at work. Slowly, he was becoming less and less himself and more and more "Maeve's boyfriend." I knew Zeke too well and realized that he could only be outside of his daily routine for a short amount of time before he fell apart like a house of cards.

Zeke called me late one night, exhausted and panic stricken. He had not done notes on a script that was due the next day and he was supposed to be at Maeve's in a few hours. He did not want to skip out on Maeve; he was smitten, the sex was insanely good, and he thought she was the woman he would marry. However, if he didn't do the work he could lose his job.

He was actually scared to call Maeve and cancel their plans for the evening. It is important to set boundaries, especially time limits, early on; and I told Zeke what a big step in their relationship this evening was. He had to let Maeve know that he could not always be there and that sometimes his friends or work had to come first. By doing this, they would avoid confusion and heartache further down the road when all of a sudden he was taking a ton of time for himself to go to the gym and see his own friends.

Unfortunately, Zeke did not take any "me" time for himself that night. He continued the pattern of minimal sleep and slave-like attention to Maeve's livelihood. Inevitably he had a breakdown and took it out on her, screaming and throwing a tantrum saying, "I need my space! I need my space!" Maeve was confused, obviously. He had never "needed his space" before. Luckily, they worked it out. They have put off moving in together and Zeke has gone back to making sure he goes to the bathroom at the same time every day and gets adequate sleep. Maeve has finally gotten some breathing room too. Now she has plenty of time to have sex with her hot boss. She has time to do it, but she doesn't. Bobby and I just fuck with Zeke and tell him that she does. What she really does is go to movies with friends and probably has a little opportunity to actually miss Zeke.

Boundaries set up early on in a relationship are important in defining who you are to your partner. Anything else is a misrepresentation. I know when I first met Carlo, I wanted to do everything for him, be with him all the time, and be the kind of person that I thought he wanted me to be. I was fooling myself; I was so lost in my passion for him that I forgot to take care of myself. The longer it went on, the longer it took to recover from it and remember the things I liked to do and needed to do to survive.

I sacrificed a lot during the first year of our relationship. He liked my cooking so I cooked almost every night, which was not me. I love to cook but I ran out of ideas after a few months. It would have been better to have limited the home-cooking to a couple of times a week so he had something to look forward to. As it was, he grew to expect gourmet cuisine every night of the week.

He didn't like cussing and I think I only heard him use swear words maybe twice in our entire relationship. I cuss so much I think I invented half of the curse words I use. For him, I stifled myself and cussed very little. That was not me either. One day I exploded and they all came shooting out like a machine gun. I finally had to stop always thinking about what Carlo wanted and take back control of my life. I had a lot of catching up to do. I had writing projects to complete and old friends to see, if they would still have me. I do not regret any aspects of the relationship with Carlo, though, I had a great time falling in love and losing myself. I was able to recover the parts of myself that I sacrificed but some people never snap out of it and set up those boundaries. They live as a couple, taking no time for themselves. When this happened to a couple I knew, Devon and Amanda, Jasmine started calling them by a new name, "Demanda."

Some people I know have no boundaries when it comes to time spent in relationships because they have been waiting their entire lives for just that opportunity to become someone's something. My friend Debbie is a perfect example of this. She has wanted a husband since she was a little girl and was ready to be completely devoted to the right person. She finally met and fell in love with a man whom she did everything for. She took care of his dogs and dropped everything, including her family and career, for him. She ended up moving to the country to help him run his horse ranch. They just had a baby and Debbie could not be happier. An ex-musician, she would rather play guitar to her kids than pursue a music career. If her

Katie Moran

husband told her that guitar playing bothered him, she would probably throw it out the window. Her only priority in life is being a wife and mother; she has no boundaries in what she will do to maintain that. This is her new identity, the one she had hoped for.

Some boundaries are jealousy driven. Before Carlo and I started dating he was with a very jealous, manipulative woman. He was scared of losing her because she constantly threatened that she would leave if he did not follow all of her rules. This woman hated Carlo's first cat. Now, I hated Carlo's second cat, Stacie, but I would never have asked him to get rid of her for me. I know I would never give up my dog for any man, or woman; I would be offended if a partner even suggested it. His ex asked him to give away his cat and Carlo reluctantly sent it, his best little friend, to live with his sister. When he broke up with the woman, he went up north to retrieve his cat but the animal never forgave him. After a month, a car hit the cat and Carlo never forgave himself for sending him away in the first place.

Carlo's ex also insisted that he get rid of his best friend from childhood, a female, of course. He did and he told me that his friend cried on the phone and could not understand why. Luckily after the break-up, Carlo's best friend was not mad at him for the way he had brushed her aside. They are great friends now and she is actually one of my good friends, too. She was never a threat to me, unlike with Carlo's ex who was acting out of jealousy and insecurity. Carlo, in turn, was not strong enough to set boundaries in his relationship with this woman.

There are some boundaries that are important in structuring a life with someone you care about. Mia was awoken night after night by girls calling her new boyfriend. He was one of the hottest young bachelors in LA so it was no surprise that these girls kept pursuing him. Even after she had moved into his house, the succession of phone calls was never-ending. She would answer the phone and girls would blatantly ask her if they could come over. When she was out with him women would push her out of the way to throw their cleavage, and their phone numbers, at him. He never took the phone calls but he did bask in all the attention. She caught him smirking in bed one night, as he lay there listening to one girl on his answering machine cry and profess her love to him, and then relay all of the filthy and fantastic things she would do to him if she ever came to LA and saw him again. Mia jumped up and hit "erase" on the machine.

What Mia really wanted to do was "erase" his entire past. She was done with her boyfriend's black book that had literally come alive and spilled into her ears night after night. She told him how distressing the calls were and set a boundary with him that night. She wanted to give him an ultimatum and tell him to "change his phone number or else" but knew that such demands often lead to resentments in the future. Instead, she asked him to do the dirty work himself. From that point on, he answered every phone call and told the ladies, in the nicest possible way, that he was off the market. He would say, "I have a girlfriend now and I am in love with her. Please do not call me anymore." If they continued to call, they would block the girl's number. He did have to change his mobile phone because Mia was not ready to trust him completely; she had to have some reassurance.

Recently, to Mia's relief, she and her now fiancé moved to a different area code so the number had to change. And when a man hits on her in front of her fiancé, she proudly takes her man by the hand and says, "I am with him . . . but thanks anyway."

As the relationship progresses, the list of boundaries tends to grow longer and more serious. Add marriage, children, and more responsibilities and we could be here all day discussing

Katie Moran

these factors. It takes respecting oneself and valuing a partner to work with these rules and requests.

Now I remember to keep my boundaries fair and appropriate. I make sure that by limiting my partner I am not limiting myself. I keep an open mind and hear my partner out before making any decisions. I maintain my identity and time for myself without growing overcome with selfishness. Well, most of the time I do all of this. There are times when I slip and scream out, "Don't ever burp in my face again or I will fucking bitch slap you down to Mexico, jerk-off!" Then I come to my senses and realize what is excusable and what is not. And because I have done the inexcusable myself, I am now far more forgiving of what was previously intolerable.

12

FQ

y brother introduced me to the FQ concept several years ago. It is a system of rating the sex appeal of any given person by assigning a score between 1 and 100 called the FQ, or fuckability quotient. For example, rock stars have a really high FQ; Kid Rock may have a face like a prison rat but his FQ is in the high nineties due to his rock star status, body, and overall image. He fits perfectly with love Pam Anderson, high on the FQ chart for her famously round faux breasts, blond hair, and *Baywatch* beach bod. The FQ is best determined in relation to another person; the FQ is a relative measurement, as one person's idea of what is worthy of fucking could be totally different than their best friend's.

Look at couples and see how their sex appeal relates to one another to determine FQ. Obviously, a straight guy would look at a hot gay man and say that he has no FQ points while much of the population would strongly disagree. There are several factors that go into determining FQ points, like physical appearance, intelligence, sense of humor, amiability, social or financial status, overall appeal to the opposite (or same) sex, and how they relate to that one special person. Other factors that I hear can bump up someone's FQ rating and make them more fuck worthy is how they interact with children (the ever-popular "he would make a good dad" appeal) or, for a woman, her willingness to experiment sexually.

I asked Zeke whom he, out of two women, would grant a higher FQ rating. The first contestant was a blonde from Malibu who looked like good wife material. She was from a great family, dressed and smelled great, was funny and nice to all of his friends, and wanted to have children. Contestant number two was also a blonde, but from Hollywood, dressed hot and smelled even hotter, could care less if she ever saw a child cross her path, was funny yet vile, was a bitch to some of his friends, and would take it up the ass at any given time. Zeke rated contestant number two ten points higher than contestant number one because, after all, sex appeal is about sex. It is not about marriage and family. Although some people I know are turned on sexually by someone's familial qualifications.

Two of the guys I dated, Austin and Danny, had comparable levels of sex appeal. Both were half Italian and great in bed, although Austin was slightly better. Both were athletic and good-looking, although Austin had a better body. But Danny had that East Coast charm and Austin had very little in the personality department. Ultimately, I would rate Austin about four points higher, a 96, while I would rate Danny a 92. I think if Austin called me today and asked for sex I would be there with open arms and open legs.

I would consider having sex with Danny again but most likely I would just meet him for a drink and ride piggyback around the bar with him, making jokes and catching up on old times. I would have an equally good time with either one of them, as I can have just as much fun having good sex as I can laughing my ass off in a bar. Austin just had that quiet brooding thing that is only seen in the old-time actors like James Dean. He was the guy sitting at the end of that coffee shop counter by himself, lost in thought. And a guy who knows when to keep his mouth shut can really turn on women.

And, then there is someone like, oh, I don't know, Meg Ryan. I imagine she is quite a catch—she is very pretty, sweet, and charming—but when I think of her I don't think of sex. I can't imagine her naked, and I really don't want to. I would be scared that if I went down on her she would start giggling or something. She just has a lower FQ; of course, some may disagree. I think sex appeal comes from something deep down inside. Like dick size, sex appeal can be seen through the eyes. I know how to spot the tigers nowadays and I always seem to find the really aggressive and passionate lovers.

When I go out with Talia, she is looking for something altogether different. She looks for someone sweet and gentle. She likes men who take all night; she enjoys all of the little things that go into romance and that can happen very slowly. I like people who want it so bad they cannot wait. I guess I would be very bad practicing tantric sex. My reality of a situation may be completely different than someone else's but we can all agree on one—Angelina Jolie. One hundred percent FQ rating at all times! The majority of straight woman would have sex with Angelina if they could only have one lesbian experience. She is the end all. I know the movie *Gia* converted a significant number of seemingly straight young women into active bisexuals. One of these is Jasmine. She said that seeing Angelina Jolie's character naked and glowing the morning after she and her girlfriend have just had sex for the first time changed her forever. The

Katie Moran

vulnerability in Angelina's eyes coupled with the curves of her amazing figure captured the attention of many female viewers.

After seeing *Gia,* Jasmine wanted to have sex with Angelina so bad that she went out looking for her first female lover. Angelina Jolie is sexy because she is not afraid to talk about sex. She has animal-like prowess. She is beautiful and my friends who have interviewed her or hung out with her say she is a genuine person with a heart of gold. And forget about everyone who calls her crazy . . . 99 percent of people living in Los Angeles are insane. Whether the craziness is caused by the bad air quality or the superficiality of life here is anyone's guess.

People in LA are focused on looks and wealth and getting ahead at any cost. I remember going to New Orleans on vacation and getting rear-ended in my rental car by a girl from Alabama who was going fifty. My LA training took hold of me and I started yelling and grabbed my camera to collect evidence. She just looked at me and said, "Sorry, y'all. I was lookin' through my purse for some make-up and didn't see y'all. So sorry 'bout this." She completely disarmed me. I have noticed during my subsequent travels through the South that people are different there; they are honest and have manners. That, to me, is sexy.

When it comes to your sex life the goal is to find someone with the same FQ as you. My brother claims people who do not have the same FQ are not sexually compatible. In general, strippers are really sexy but may not be overly intelligent, educated, or even good-looking but, wow, are they fuckable. In my early twenties I was very taken with strippers; their fake names and breasts, their cat-like movements around a pole. The first lap dance I ever had was when I was twenty-three. I took Aunt Julia to a local strip club with the word "classy" in the name and it was anything but. Thank God! My grandfather had given us $50 to do what we wanted and we chose to go see strippers, which we knew he would have approved of.

The "On" Position

The first one to get a dance was Aunt Julia. After ten minutes she came out of the little room behind a black curtain, lighting a cigarette with a geeky look on her face. She sat down, clearly delirious and affected. I said, "Well, how was it?" thinking that maybe it was a disappointment. She just looked at me with eyes as wide as saucers and grin quickly spreading across her face and said, "That was the best damn twenty bucks I have ever spent in my entire life! You got to do it!"

So I did. My experience getting a lap dance was a little different than hers. The stripper, a tiny blonde girl who could wrap her legs around the back of her neck, took a liking to me. She began biting the inside of my thigh and then ripped my top off, sucking on my nipples. I was in shock. I said, "I thought there was no touching?" I had my hands tucked tightly under my ass so I would not have the urge to fondle her. She shyly said, "Not for you" and took both of my hands and rubbed them across her entire body up and down for three songs. It was the best simulated sex I have ever had. Strippers are sexy but why wouldn't they be? They sell sex for a living. Even more than that, they sell the fantasy. Only a rare few of us take that fantasy home. A life of living the fantasy is the kind that I want to lead.

A couple of years later I was at my friend Robin's new condo. She was Entertainer of the Year at the gentleman's club she worked at during this time. She wanted me to meet her new roommate, a girl named Roberta. When Roberta came out of her room I recognized her as the stripper who had gently molested me a few years ago. Roberta was a much less-flattering name than her stripper name, which was Crystal or Shyla or something of that nature. Roberta was so embarrassed to see me that she ran back into her bedroom. It turns out it wasn't our encounter in the dark room at the back of the strip club that ashamed her; she was embarrassed because she didn't have all her make-up on!

Katie Moran

Without the make-up, costumes, and glamour, strippers are just regular girls. That is probably why they date so many musicians. Musicians create the same kind of illusion when they are up on stage, wearing leather pants and make-up, shiny guitar or drumsticks in hand. No matter how broke, dim, and ugly a dude is, if he has an amazing voice and can wail on a guitar, his FQ goes way up. I doubt there are too many struggling bass players dating budding Donna Karan–wearing junior executives, but I could be wrong. There are no rules, no wrongs or rights of who can fuck whom. And sexy can be found anywhere.

I have always felt that any person should be allowed to date or have sex with any other person without regard to race, religion, age, or sex. Of course, that doesn't mean I don't turn and stare when I see a ninety-year-old man making out with a thirty-year-old woman. There are certain oddities found in couples from time to time. I knew a guy that was about 5'5" and 120 pounds and had a 365-pound wife who absolutely towered over and fully enveloped him. So, when I met Ava and Lenore, a lesbian couple traveling the country in an RV promoting their erotic film, I kept an open mind.

Carlo had a friend, Claire, that I didn't particularly like. She was a vegan who talked really slow and hit on Carlo every time we would see her. She would hang all over him, right in front of me. Carlo and I were fighting a lot at the time and I didn't want to meet anyone related to Claire. However, that night Carlo insisted that we all go to dinner together to meet her friends. Somewhat reluctantly I agreed to meet the out-of-towners. When Ava and Lenore walked up to the Mexican restaurant in West Hollywood that night, I was immediately charmed by Ava's milk-fed country girl good looks and Lenore's forceful personality. Ava, a mild-mannered, twenty-four-year-old blonde from Maine, had a big smile and exotic blue-green eyes. Lenore was twenty years her senior, and not a bit blessed with the attractive gene, being fairly masculine and unkempt, however she seemed nice. I was shocked to find out that they were a couple. The FQ just did not match up.

Ava was about a 90, in my opinion and Lenore was about, hmmm, a big zero on my scale. I couldn't believe someone so hot would be dating someone so, well . . . not. I thought perhaps Lenore was rich and Ava was a gold digger but Lenore didn't seem to be particularly wealthy. In fact, she looked as if she had played hopscotch on the trashy side of the schoolyard. I just couldn't see the attraction there. They looked like the oddest couple, kind of a mother and daughter thing. I thought, "But Lenore is nice, maybe that's it . . . or maybe Ava has a mommy thing," which I came to find out that she did. She and her mother had a strained relationship and Ava's abandonment issues with women had driven her into the arms of this caretaker type. Lenore spent a good part of the evening talking about herself and her budding career as a pornographer. She had financed her first movie and was looking for distribution. And publicity. I guess that is where I came into play.

I think Lenore was hoping I would do a story or a review for one of the various sex mags I write for. I wasn't interested and didn't have the time. Then Ava mentioned that she was the star of the movie and it was her first film. My boyfriend and I almost coughed up our margaritas and both looked at her and said in unison, "YOU are in the movie?" Now I was listening. Ava nodded. We promised to go right home and watch it that night. We did. I was immediately turned on by Ava after seeing her perform sexually in this movie.

Carlo encouraged me to befriend Ava because we had so much in common, or so it seemed. She and I were both around the same age and loved dogs and fast cars. My boyfriend and I felt bad for her because she was trapped in this trailer with the overbearing Lenore. The two of them shared one car and Lenore would never let Ava out of her sight. She pretended she

Katie Moran

was fine with Ava sleeping with other women and having freedom, but the truth was that she kept her on a tight leash, controlling the amount of money she had access to and whom she was able to hang out with. I also realized that Ava had a choice; she was a heavy drinker and partier who preferred this lazy lifestyle.

Ava was such an addict that she would rather be with this horrid woman, living in a pigsty than go to work or pursue her own dreams. She had had a full ride to one of the best colleges in the country and yet had failed out after a year. She partied her education away and now was putting tacky tattoos on her body where her girlfriend told her to and taking pills. She went from Ivy League to porn dyke in a matter of a year. Carlo and I thought there was a chance she might snap out of it one day and that we could help her.

I spoke to Bobby about Ava and Lenore. He had trouble remembering people's names because so many of his friends came to him with relationship advice. He asked if we could please refer to them from here on out as "the pussy" and "the dog." I asked him why some beautiful women like "the pussy" ruin their lives and end up with mates like "the dog" that are far below them. Was it a self-esteem issue? Bobby said, "Maybe, honey. But you and I both know we have never had to fuck ugly before and I hope to God we never will!"

I know it sounds as if I am putting Lenore, "the dog," down and that I am being caddy. In the months to follow, she proved to me that her insides matched the outside. She was not a nice person, had no scruples, and used each and every person she met along her journey through Los Angeles until she was finished with them, and then tossed them aside. I helped her out for about three weeks until her phone calls, demands, and requests became a complete nuisance. I decided to see what would happen if I didn't do all the favors she asked for. She stopped calling and stopped inviting me over. She was very predictable.

I think the thing that bothered me the most was how sweet and nice (and gullible) her girlfriend acted. I remember one day sitting over at their motor home (yes, they never did reach stardom and move out of a tin box) and meeting a man that had come up with a brilliant invention. He did not have the money to patent the idea and he told this to Lenore. She asked my advice and I told her to go into business with him and finance his idea. Instead, she went behind his back and patented the idea, stealing it and passing it off as her own. At that point, I knew she was truly ugly. Ava continued to stay around and was completely gaga over her. They would always brag about their sex life and how they stayed up all night and morning, fucking until 9 AM. Those were the moments when I would start balancing my checkbook in my head or go over all the stuff I had to get at the grocery store for my grandma. Who wants to picture an ugly person having sex? I don't.

If it were someone with high FQ like Gwen Stefani talking about having sex with Angelina Jolie, sure, I would listen. But when the person talking about female ejaculation is a dirty chick with buck teeth who practically has a bandana growing out of her head I want to puke. In my mind I was singing "LA LA LA LA LA LA LA" the way you do when you are a kid and you tune out everything your mom is saying.

People like Lenore earn their zero points on the FQ scale; they are not just cursed with them due to their monstrous looks. She was one of those highly manipulative people who are not intelligent enough to carry it off. It just came off as blatant rudeness. She would say things like, "I know you are a girl with high character and someone who is trusting and generous. That is why I know you will loan me your house for the weekend while you are out of town."

Katie Moran

My only reply was, "Yes, I do have a high character and you still can't borrow my house."

I did not want her trashy filth all over my place. I cannot even imagine the nerve of someone I have known for two months asking to stay in my place! One time she insisted upon showing me a video of her and her drunken girlfriend having sex. They clearly confused female ejaculation with urination. I know the difference. Their idea of good sex was basically just to pee all over each other's sagging bodies.

Before I knew how scandalous Lenore was I took my friend Kristina out to drinks with her and Ava. Kristina had way too much to drink and Lenore encouraged her to smoke as much weed as possible, later complaining that everyone smokes her stuff. Kristina was slightly attracted to the half-decent Ava and hopped in bed with her at around four in the morning, when she felt she had no other options. Lenore was there but Kristina said she tried to ignore her presence. Kristina had read *The Sexual Life of Catherine M* one too many times and was convinced that dabbling on the dark side of sex (i.e., sleeping with someone dirty and repulsive without judgment) was freeing and fashionable.

I think the beauty of Catherine M is that she viewed every man with some kind of equality, despite his physical prowess or cleanliness. Kristina tried to adopt this point of view but she was from the South Bay, after all, and her idea of filth is spilling too much beer on your tits and getting too much sand between your toes. Obviously, she reported to me later, the experience with the trailer trash duo was disgusting and unsatisfying. She said every time she opened her eyes, Lenore had one less item of clothing left on until she was lying there panting and drooling over the girls like a wrinkled leech.

I cannot fathom having sex when something or someone looks grotesque or smells rank. Sex is an all-senses-present activity for me. Everything contributes to the outcome: the way someone's laundry detergent smells; the way someone's soft skin feels, and the way their environment looks. Carlo and I were a good sensory match; he and I were no supermodels, but we got by just fine. He was a little older than I was but he also made more money than I did. He and I were both creative types and enjoyed the same kinds of activities. We traveled frequently and loved the ocean. He loved to sail and I loved to water-ski and Jet Ski. We were kindred spirits and our FQ similarities drew us to one another. It is so sexy to be seduced by someone you love, someone who smells clean and good enough to eat, in a dark, warm room with a fireplace and candles, and great music playing.

Sex can be exciting for me when it is uncomfortable but only if it all adds up in the end. Maybe having sex against a balcony rail overlooking the Gulf of Mexico is cold and rough, but there is still an overall beauty to it. Perhaps having sex in a cheesy club with plastic seats and people wearing tacky stripper gear does it for you, but I have yet to meet one person that likes to perform oral sex on someone with a dirty and rank mass down there.

This is how I anticipate sex with Lenore must be. I was so disturbed by the visual Kristina described to me that I could not even have sex with Carlo for weeks. Things of a sexual nature affect me deeply, crawling into my veins, my subconscious, and my nerve endings until I can feel the way someone might have felt or seen what they had to see. This also works in reverse and when I hear of an enticing sexual encounter I can use that image to enhance my own sex life. When sex with Carlo grew boring from its frequency and lack of atmosphere change, I could easily visualize and become a participant in a fantasy of the mind.

As far as "the pussy" and "the dog's" FQs were concerned, Ava's began to drop more and more each time I saw her. She was falling right down there with her partner. They were

Katie Moran

becoming even more compatible as a couple. The pornography life of drinks, pills, and sex had taken over. Ava looked grotesque to me now; life in a dirty motor home had not treated her well. Plus, all of my friends who met the couple agreed that knowing that Ava was stooping to have sex with someone as repulsive as Lenore dropped her down about 20 points on the FQ scale. Like the old saying, if you sleep with pigs, you become one. And if you sleep with a bull-dyke-drug-addict-pornographer, you become that too.

What is your FQ? Do you walk around oozing sex appeal? Can lovers barely keep their hands off you or are they waiting for you to make the first move for fear of mussing the crease in your wool skirt? Are you stared down at coffee shops, other patrons' mouths gaping open in yearning, or are you more of a "get to know you" type of guy or gal? Rate yourself: Determine your own FQ and write down potential lovers that fall into the same category as yourself. For example, I think my FQ fits really well with that of hockey players. I don't know why but it just seems that a young, blond, LA writer goes really well with the sex appeal of an ice-smashing athlete. Why? Because I want it to, damn it!

I believe the sexiness I exude in my own game is about the same as a man who is also good at his game . . . preferably on the ice. He does not have to be brilliant or gorgeous, just as I am not a six-foot-tall supermodel, but there has to be that element of surprise. Hockey player or not, I have to find a mate who is not offended by my lewd stories or checkered past; rather, I need one who is aroused by and interested in them. If he can forgive and love the fact that I have eaten pussy, or, in the case of a woman, if she can forgive the fact that I have had sex with a man, I can surely look past his busted nose or her extra ten pounds.

We have many sides to our personalities. One aspect of who we are might allure one person while another aspect might tempt someone completely different. My active side attracts the athletic types. But I also attract and am attracted to tons of creative people because there is a mutual admiration in those that share the artists' lifestyle. It is not just because we cannot be reached until noon because we are sleeping or are often seen having lunch at four in the afternoon because we are out of work, it is the way our minds work and how we feel we have no other options than to create.

My friend Clay is a vegetarian. He shops at Whole Foods daily, re-using his canvas sacks and stocking up on flax seed. One day he met the girl of his dreams in the check-out line and he claims she is the most fuck-worthy woman in the world. I am not particularly attracted to her; she wears organic gauze clothing and has a weird sage and oatmeal odor. But they are so attracted to each other and together, watching them interact, I realized that they are both a perfect 100 on their own FQ scales.

I know a middle-aged couple, friends of my mom's and former neighbors. They are both certified public accountants for huge corporations. By now, they are probably CFOs or directors of tax, but I know little about accounting, so I won't pretend I bothered finding out exactly what they do. However, I do know they are the hottest geeks I have ever met. They are both tall and sexy, keeping in shape by skiing at their vacation home all winter. When tax time rolls around they abstain from sex, choosing numbers over nudity. They are locked in front of their computer screens, black horn-rimmed glasses tightly hugging their faces. They admit to going to bed late and choosing to sleep in separate bedrooms because the stress level is so high they do not want anyone to touch them. Yet when the summer sun burns hot in the sky, they both share the same love of beach time with their kids in Newport.

My friend Hank is one of the most self-deprecating people I have ever met—yet he and his wife Ashley are so in love.

Katie Moran

Though most people would find them unattractive, they are perfect for each other. They have compatible fuckability quotients because only they get each other, no one else does. Recently their weights have been climbing and Hank's wife has been thinking seriously about getting pregnant. She says, "Why not, I am already fat. Might as well have people think it is because I am pregnant instead of just eating too many In 'n' Out burgers!" I could not help but laugh. I think Ashley is a very sexy girl who just works too much. By the time she gets home from work it is after eight and all she wants to do is go to bed. Cooking healthy is the furthest thing from her mind so she and her husband fall prey to fast food more often than not.

Hank said, "I bet our baby will be really cute." I looked at him strangely, not wanting to question that assumption but also realizing that his wife has one of those single-file type faces where her eyes are so close together they line up with her almost-invisible mouth. Hank thinks it's adorable. Before I could say anything on the cute baby comment, Ashley quickly added, "Because ugly people always have the prettiest babies!" Only Ashley could put herself down like that and not cry about it later when she was alone. She accepted that she was no Cindy Crawford (although we were like most girls in high school who pretended that we were going to be that hot one day) and moved on with her life, meeting her future husband at the age of twenty.

Celebrity couples such as ex-flames Ben Affleck and Jennifer Lopez, media whores extraordinaire, are on equal footing when it comes to their sex appeal. Most girls I know would have sex with Ben, but he would not be their first choice of actors to have sex with. And most guys I know might have sex with J.Lo., although they would probably want to tape her mouth shut. Their FQ is about an even 70 to me; neither one is someone I would ever be attracted to. Blonde cuties Reese Witherspoon and Ryan Phillippe are too adorable for words. They have even bred and produced perfect little blonde replicas of themselves. They also have earning power and a great deal of talent—they match perfectly on the FQ scale. Maybe that is why they met and fell in love at such an early age; if looks and likeability had anything to do with their romance, I am sure they both knew it was a winning combination from the beginning.

It is no secret that I have this thing for Stevie Nicks. I think she is so sexy and that she and I would be very compatible. Okay, so she makes a ton more money than I do and she is nearly thirty years older, but she looks damn good for her age and hey, maybe she would appreciate a younger woman. Or, maybe I am just dreaming. Few people my age even know what band she is in let alone understand my freakish obsession with her. I never miss a show and I remember being at a concert in San Diego and standing in one of the first few rows, but I was the only person dancing. I felt like she spotted me and smiled. In my mind, it was as cool as if we had danced together.

This is how crazy stalkers must think except they really believe it is true. I was not being delusional; I just kind of let myself live in the fantasy for a song or two. There is nothing wrong with that, right? This girl I was sleeping with could imitate Stevie's voice perfectly. We would do a little role-playing; she would play Stevie and I would play a groupie. Then, we would have wild groupie sex to an old Fleetwood Mac album. She would pretend to be a really reluctant rock legend, too busy to deal with me. Then, I would seduce her after a "show" and she would croon in ecstasy. After that, we would both laugh hysterically and go back to being ourselves. Fantasies are fun even when you are absolutely certain they will never happen in real life.

Enacting fantasies can be sexy, but there is a fine line between sexy and scary. Carlo always thought it would be really hot to sleep with someone who was a little wacko. I asked him,

Katie Moran

"Aren't I crazy enough for you? I stole someone's disposable camera at a Fourth of July barbecue last week and took pictures of Bobby's butt hole then put it back so that the owner of the camera would develop it. That's nuts!" It was not exactly what he was talking about.

This was more like it: When we were in Hawaii I pretended to be a crazy vagabond professional surfer and he would play the part of a traveling businessman. He would reluctantly bring surfer girl back to his room where she would attempt to steal from him. They would have sex anyway and then the surfer girl would move on, only to meet again months later. This backfired when we temporarily broke up. Carlo met a psycho snowboarding chick while on a ski trip in Colorado. He said he had trouble shaking the girl once they had slept together. He found out that she had no place to go and made it a habit of bed hopping during ski season. He said he knew there was a major problem when he woke up in the morning to find her dressed head to toe in his ski clothes. When dating enters the *Twilight Zone*, it is time to run the other way.

Bobby was back on the dating scene and really believed he would find the "one" this time. So, he went to the place all gay guys go to find a quality man, a bathhouse. Bobby cruised the block on Melrose where the bathhouse was located. He went around and around, debating whether or not to go in or just go back home and watch *Friends* re-runs. He saw his future husband (or so he thought) walk out, looking freshly showered. Bobby decided if that is what the "spa" had to offer, he was going to be a member. He could not find a parking space so he offered to drive the hot guy to his Range Rover and take his spot. The man was an older exec type and he blatantly looked Bobby's young body up and down.

They sat in the parking lot for a half hour before making up their minds to take the flirtation to the next level. Bobby skipped going to the spa and took Roman's invitation to have a private massage back at his place. He knew that this guy was off the FQ charts. He was gorgeous, he ran ten miles a day, and he owned his own house, yacht and plane. You would think a guy like Roman would have a boyfriend, right? Bobby and I both knew that most near-perfect guys had boyfriends. And this one did. He neglected to tell Bobby about his significant other, and when Bobby confronted Roman about it, he passed his lover off as his "on again, off again" ex. These are risky. Either you are on or you are off, which one is it? It was obviously not over. Bobby had his heart broken for the third time this year. At least Bobby's FQ rating went up when he dated Roman. Every queen in West Hollywood saw them together and gave Bobby major props for landing this stud.

Some people feel the need to date outside of their FQ—this leads them right into the arms of loneliness. I have a friend named Kenny who is an average-looking guy; a little on the chubby side, and still has a roommate at thirty-nine years old. Kenny's career is not taking off the way he had planned; he has plenty of nice women who would go out on a date with him but he thinks he can land any girl he wants. When he goes out he ignores the women who have an FQ rating similar to his, rather, he hits on every other twenty-something he meets. They just look at him in bewilderment over the top of their Grey Goose martinis; drinks that he couldn't even afford to buy them. He is a buddy of mine and I am glad he feels so positive about his prospects. But sometimes I wish he would come back down to reality because then he might actually find happiness. He hit on Jasmine more than once, thinking that she might like to be picked up in his broken-down car and go Dutch at the movies. He is literally the guy who has women laugh in his face. Except for hookers; they love him.

Who has the same FQ as you? Just for fun, next time you are out and about and someone catches your eye, ask yourself if they have the same fuckability quotient as you. Watch for the

Katie Moran

recognition in their eyes, the equality, and the familiarity. Make a move and let nature take its course. It is really fun when you find out you have met your match. An exercise such as this one will also help move you one step closer to recognizing and nailing down the person that you want.

13

Doors

Growing up, I was always told that when one door closes another one opens. For example, you get fired from your job and end up landing one that pays more money or is more gratifying. Hopefully, in relationships, when the door shuts on a person who was not working out, another will open and welcome in someone better. I have always been a person who has trouble closing the door on past relationships. Post break-up, I often end up sleeping with my ex for a year or so. Even worse, I end up being their best friend and am forced to listen to the horrors of their new relationship. Maybe it is fear; I am afraid of losing something or being alone. I want to have the door left open just a crack so I can peek in and maybe jump back on the other side when times get tough.

A girl I know kept the door open for an ex who moved

overseas. Nearly ten years later, he moved back to the States, they married, and just had their first child. Some doors are worth keeping open. However, sometimes you don't have a choice. I have had doors slammed shut in my face by people who get married or who just plain don't want to be with me. Some doors shut slowly, so gradually that the feelings disappear over a period of time. And when you turn your head to look back, miraculously, the feelings are gone. Funny isn't it, that when you stop caring for someone you may have been crazy about in the past, they seem to pop back into your life, shoving their foot through that crack in the door, forcing an entry.

Call it breaking and entering, but when I began dating Shada, another hot blonde, blue-eyed chick with huge boobs (hey, it used to be my type), all of our slightly open doors swung open and the ugly contents dumped themselves on our doorstep right at the beginning of what could have been a really cool relationship. Shada had three exes whom she still spoke to, doors that were still cracked open so she could peek around. The first one was the open-door ex-fiancé who still had some of her clothes in his closet, an un-worn wedding band in a dresser drawer, and a wallet full of cash waiting to go into her purse the day she needed to come back. After two years of waiting, he finally confronted her—three weeks after I met her. Bad timing, to say the least. Now she had to go through the grieving of a break-up that should have taken place years prior.

Then there was her ex Michael. Shada had been madly in love with him and he had never returned the feelings. They talked and occasionally had sex before she and I met. Remember, we were only a few weeks into this dating thing and it was already completely uncomfortable with the first ex! Now Michael was calling incessantly and wanting to see her and I was now intercepting phone calls. The strange thing was that I think she enjoyed his attention and admitted that his undying devotion was all she had ever really wanted. And now he was offering it to her and she clearly wanted to take it. She did not want to be with him but she definitely wanted to wallow in his attention and his sudden passion for her. She had never closed the door on him because she lived with the hope that he would change. He did—as soon as she was with me and unavailable.

You'd think that was enough, but there is more. The third was a guy she had had sex with only three times but because he was an alcoholic, and she had a soft spot for emotionally sick men, she was attached and at his beck and call. He was the "swinging door" ex. She kept going back and forth and back and forth again. The swinging door is a door that can never close. This happens frequently when there is a child involved in the relationship. The door stays open because the two partners are forced to see each other on a regular basis. If there are feelings added to the mix, the door never stops moving. One minute she may never want to see him and the next she may be planning to elope with him. He would go on boozing sprees and call her on a comedown. She would be there to baby him and pick up the pieces of his shattered life. Although they were now supposedly just "friends," I knew that it was one door I wanted to kick shut—in his face!

Already, Shada and I were doomed as a couple. I was barely an extra in the drama she was starring in. Yet I was not free from all blame. My ex Jasmine and I would still talk on a daily basis and have these occasional make-out sessions that were intense and spontaneous. I found it impossible to not return her phone calls or to stop seeing her due to our amicable break-up. We did not break up out of anger or hurt; it just wasn't going anywhere, but we still liked each other. So, the door remains open. For me, it was a safety net, something to call home when the insanity set in with Shada.

Another ex, someone who I had always wished would dump

his tired girlfriend and come running back to me, did. One day while at Shada's house, this guy called me crying and wanting to spend every day with me. I still loved him but I had already shut the door and moved on without even being aware of it. I no longer had the same feelings for him. I became even more confused and frustrated because I liked being around him but I wasn't attracted to him anymore. Call it self-protection, but I had become guarded. Plus, I had already moved on to Shada.

So, there I was, wrapped up in the commotion with Shada, and I was so addicted to wanting what I could not have that there was little room for even the most perfect offer. She and I seemed screwed and we most likely were. The mature thing to do would have been to write her a letter calling it off so that we could both deal with the messes of our past. I did the letter-writing part, but did I give it to her? Hell, no! I optimistically waited around hoping something would change for the better.

It is almost three years since Shada and I had our first kiss. It was the night of my birthday party and I leaned in nervously, not knowing if she would even accept it. I held her against a wall, and we looked at each other in the eyes, rather than close them like you do when you actually trust someone. My signals from her were so mixed that I wanted to see with my own eyes if she would actually let me kiss her. She did, and our teeth clanked against each other. It was awful!

It took about a month but then I closed the door on Shada. We remained friends but I realized it was useless to consider developing feelings for her. Sometimes we are able to close doors better than our partners. Shada called me two and a half years later and admitted to having feelings for me, but only for a week. The door was so glued shut by that time I just laughed. She looked perplexed but started giggling too, realizing that we were friends, she liked men more than women, and it would not work with us, just like it did not work the first time around.

Breaking up with Carlo was the equivalent of closing a

gigantic antique solid oak door. It took two hands, all my mind power, and an occasional kick in the pants by one of my friends. I missed him so much after we broke up. I knew it was for the best, but it was really painful and lonely. He had become my best friend and I still loved him—I still love him. He had not done wrong by me; I just knew that loving myself meant not being with him anymore. It was a disservice to us both to continue seeing each other. We both wanted different things and what we did have in common did not seem to bond us together as strongly as it had in the past. There was nothing pulling us together anymore; love was just not enough.

Once we broke up, I saw a glimpse of what it was like on the other side of our relationship: the single life. After that, there was no turning back. I had a lick of freedom and wanted a whole scoop.

Carlo and I broke up for good after one of his drinking binges. I told myself if he ever drank again, in the manner he was accustomed to, the strange early-morning-closet-case drinking, I would tell him it was over. One morning I woke up with an empty feeling. I had a baby shower to go to that day for one of my stripper friends. On my way to the shower, I left a message for Carlo telling him that I was coming over that night, like I did several times a week, to have dinner and just be together. With Carlo, it never mattered what we did as long as we were together. He never called back. It was a familiar feeling, the feeling that Carlo was choosing alcohol over me. I have dated heavy partiers before, who have thrown up or passed out right in front of me. Hey, I have even been one of those kinds of partners. This was different.

Carlo would drink straight from the bottle and hide out like a recluse, skipping out on all previous commitments. I did not hear from Carlo until two days later. He had been drinking, just as suspected. My friends were less supportive when I called them and told them what was going on. They had heard this

Katie Moran

same story so many times before. Jasmine was the first to say to me, "This is the thirtieth time this has happened. He is never going to change." I kept going back and it was not getting better. Carlo would have a drinking spell every two to three weeks. This was not what I signed up for and he was not the person I fell in love with. I had given him nine months of chances to seek help but he had only gotten worse. I was done this time because finishing things with us was the best thing I could do for myself. I had lost trust that Carlo would ever be well.

As our relationship deteriorated so did our sex life. The first thing to go was my passion for Carlo; at times I cringed when he touched me. This was a guy who I once could not keep my hands off of but the stress of our problems had turned us into best friends who occasionally fooled around. The intensity of our sex and the magnetism of our lovemaking were almost totally absent. I felt bad for Carlo and I worried about myself. I was concerned that it would never come back for me, not with him and not with anyone else. I wondered if I had lost my sex drive. I did not know how to get it back. I looked at other men and the thought of having sex with them repulsed me. I wanted Carlo. Even the idea of having a fun affair with a beautiful woman did not interest me; I still wanted to want Carlo.

Doors in relationships often relate to emotions, not just people. My friend Michelle suspected part of my problem was the book-writing process; I agreed that talking about sex, thinking about sex, and writing about sex much more than the average person had made it lose its mystique for me. I had taken the luster out of my own sex life! I knew about a thousand tips and techniques for great sex but no longer knew how to just feel sex rather than think sex. I had become clinical instead of creative and had been having sex with my brain instead of my body. And my brain was not being very cooperative. I had closed the door on spontaneity.

People come to me for advice on their own sex lives. One

married friend of mine, Lisa, told me she was too tired at night to have sex with her husband. The kids and her daily life wore her down. She said thinking about sleeping eight hours would arouse her more than her husband's penis. I gave her a list of things she could try. She said she had done everything and more, the candles, the eye contact, the kissing. She even tried getting more sleep but that did not seem to help either.

One night Lisa and I were watching TV when a news report came on describing all of the ways to retrieve a woman's sex drive. One way stuck in my mind and hers. The newscaster simply said that to the best way to become re-interested in sex is to just have it. Sex is like exercise. The only way to strengthen those leg muscles is to get out and walk the first mile and both Lisa and I were out of shape sexually. I knew the answer would be found in the sex itself. All of the analysis in the world would not solve what hands-on practice could.

This worked for Lisa. I watched her kids for the weekend so she could go away and have sex with her husband. She returned from vacation with a big smile on her face. It worked. She was well rested and happy. Orgasms are great like that, aren't they? I remember seeing a girlfriend of mine after a week out of town visiting her ex and she had that same look on her face. It was a dead giveaway; they had fucked. She had the "freshly fucked" look and I had the opposite one on my face, the "freshly fucked-over" look.

After my break-up, I remembered to keep this in mind when considering dating or sleeping with someone new. I knew I had to just go for it. I had to make a move in order to get interested in having sex again. I was intimidated by the thought of getting to know someone new and taking my clothes off for someone I did knot know as well as I had known Carlo. I had gone from an aggressive sexpot to a shy wallflower. I had this and Carlo on the mind when I went out to a new club in Hollywood with Jasmine.

Katie Moran

The night out was meant to take my mind off my problems. I walked in with a sullen look on my face and slowly handed over a drink ticket to the bartender, who told me to "smile." Jasmine recommended I drink something strong, and she chose her favorite trashy Adios Mother Fucker drink for me. It was nice to say the words though, "Adios, Mother Fucker." As I drank down the electric blue embarrassment of a cocktail, I looked around the room at the sea of skin and hair products and thought, "Is THIS what is out there?" This is was the first time in two years that I had really and truly given a good and thorough look at the dating possibilities around me.

Little did I know that my future sat behind the red VIP curtain. And by future I mean three sets of gigantic breast implants pushing out from under tawdry designer tops and a thin coat of really expensive skin crème. I was single again. This time the door that opened was a curtain and I realized at that moment I could do anything I wanted to. I was not alone anymore; I was with the world.

My friend Dina says that the monotony of a relationship, the day-to-day routine is "the beauty of the beast." She finds comfort in the predictable. Perhaps I will find the truth in this one day; or maybe predictable things like drunken boyfriends will never be beautiful to me.

Jeannia, Julie, and Diana were the hottest best-friend-trio I had ever met. Their best guy friend was a comedian who immediately spotted Jasmine and pulled the two of us over to his table. He offered us drinks and Jasmine took two. As she double-fisted, the comedian said, "I saw you in a movie last night. . . . You were topless! I love your titties!" Jaz screamed and spit out the drink in her left hand.

She took a gulp from her right hand and replied, "I didn't know it was a soft-core when I did it, I swear!" The guy did not believe her but it was okay. In LA it is very forgivable, and welcomed, for a girl to show her tits to the world. Jasmine was an inadvertent skin star.

I was not worried about how we were invited into the circle that night, just that we were there and I was sitting squeezed in between the sexiest women alive. These three girls were better looking than any Playmate or any Hawaiian Tropic girl I had ever seen. They were very friendly too. I was shocked to find out that they were all in their mid-thirties, as they did not look a day over twenty-five. They all lived north of Los Angeles in the small town of Newport Beach and they informed me that they rarely went out. Jeannia took my hand, looked in my eyes and said, "When we do it, we do it BIG!" I wondered if she meant the gigantic bottle of Belvedere on the table or the two watermelons under her see-through tank top. I think she was probably referring to all of the above plus more. Those girls would not let Jaz and me go home that night. They dragged us around from bar to bar and from after-party to hotel-room party. Their guy friend confided in me that they were "cool with getting with chicks."

Ya think? Well, that was obvious. I might have not been ready for having sex after being only with Carlo for nearly two years but the door had been opened on my new life and I loved it so far. I was having fun and meeting new people, something that my relationship had not allowed for. Carlo was more of a local bar kind of guy. Jasmine and I liked to "go big" like these ladies did. I was a little rusty to the whole party scene, but I managed to hold my own until 4 AM when I finally had to bid adieu to the lovely ladies of Newport Beach. I had been such a lightweight that it took me two days to recover from the romp, even though all I had consumed was five drinks. My body was not used to so much alcohol. Nothing like my earlier days of six shots of tequila just to get started.

I was proud of myself for going out. I was back where I belonged, back in the hands of benevolent bimbos and booze.

Katie Moran

This was not simply a matter of superficial gains and temporary fun. I was back discovering what made me happy instead of what would make Carlo better. I was back in the life that I enjoyed and that had been replaced by Blockbuster nights, romantic getaways, and all of the other more intricate and complicated tasks of couple-dom. I had gone out, met some nice people, laughed my ass off, not gone too far over the edge, and not done anything I could not tell to grandma the next day. It was a small feat but it felt right. For the first time in a long while I had stopped feeling fearful about my uncertain future and just been in the moment. I never stopped thinking of Carlo, but that night I remembered how great it was to not think about anything. I let others entertain me.

It did not take me long to date after breaking up with Carlo. It certainly was not my intention to go out with anyone so soon but sometimes life just throws opportunities in front of us that are too good to pass up. One such opportunity came while I was out at a party one night in November.

Let me share with you a particularly detailed night out in Los Angeles. This is also the night that I met someone new, someone who would help me to recover my sex drive and show me who I used to love being sexually. I felt I had become more of myself in many other ways, emotionally and creatively, but I had been disappointing myself sexually.

I was headed out for a night with Jasmine and she was adamant about arriving on time for a play because the man she was in love with was the star of the show. She showed up at my place, turning off lights in my bedroom and taking my house keys off the dresser. This was my cue to hurry up. She insisted that I drive her car so she could streamline her make-up. I gladly took the chance to abuse the power of her Mercedes on the post–rush hour canyon roads. Halfway to the playhouse she realized that the play was actually the following week. Now we were all dressed up with no place to go. So typical.

I told her to call the girl she was sleeping with, a girl named Amber who had just freed herself from a three-year relationship and was hoping Jasmine was her new love. By this time, I had Jasmine all figured out. She was one of those "bisexual" women who loved to have sex with women and actually preferred it to sex with men, especially when she was drunk, but could only be emotionally entangled with a man. She would grow obsessed about guys, often upset and in tears about a man who did not respond the way she wanted him to. Simultaneously with her complete obsession for some guy, she would be combing the Internet for beautiful women to have affairs with and go to clubs with. She had more success with the girls, needless to say.

Jasmine rolled her eyes when I suggested calling Amber. She was annoyed by Amber's growing obsession to take all of Jasmine's time, time that could be better spent writing love letter novels to her "wishful-thinking boyfriend," someone that she was dating more in her own head than in real life.

The scenario with Amber sounded all too familiar. Jasmine had tricked another lesbian into falling for her by pretending she was truly a bisexual and the lesbian had, in turn, fooled Jasmine into thinking she was a bisexual and not a complete homosexual in order to score. Amber was a semi-attractive Hispanic woman of twenty-six who was in college at UCLA. She had just broken up with her sexy lover of three years, forty-year-old Margarite. We wound up at Amber's place and she fixed us a couple of drinks. She seemed sweet but I immediately could tell that all of her femininity was just a huge flirt-a-thon directed at Jasmine. Jaz is a little dim at times and I, along with other friends, have to fill her in on reality.

After a drink, I cared less about the dynamics of their sex life and more about how we were getting to the club. Amber drove and I was so excited to be out that I burst out of the car and ran

Katie Moran

through the alley behind the building in my high-heeled boots, loudly skipping my way to the door.

The night was a hit; the music was great and I danced and danced. I met the best friend of a writer whom I admired and we had a great conversation. I received many compliments from gay men on my hair, and that is always nice. There was a lot of electricity in the air. At midnight, the excitement broke and the evening turned frantic as it often does. Amber had purposely kissed Jasmine in front of Margarite to piss her off. Margarite's heart dropped and I saw tears well up in her eyes. The sadness quickly morphed into rage and she came after Amber. Amber, who is certifiably crazy (I know this now), came out swinging. Men would have paid to put these two divas in a ring. My money would have been on Margarite. It was good versus evil, and Amber was pure hatred. My vote was for good.

I could not deal with any dyke drama so I walked out on the patio. They were grown women and they could work it out themselves. Jasmine and I sat in silence. I had quit smoking years before but I often stole drags off of my friend's cigarettes during moments like this. She told me to "get my own" so I turned to a group of girls standing under a tree. One particular girl caught my eye. She was adorable. She was a tiny thing, maybe 100 pounds. She did not look old enough to be in a bar. She was so cute I wanted to hug her. She had something else in mind and she looked at me in a purposefully seductive and sexual way. I was taken aback—I was getting hit on and objectified by a fifteen-year-old! She strolled up to me and introduced herself as Stefanie. She asked me how old I was and I just looked at her as if to say "old enough to slap you across the face for even asking me that!"

I told her and she said an inconclusive, "Oh."

I asked her how old she was and she said, "Twenty-three."

I said, "No, you're not." Finally, she said, "Okay, I'm twenty."

I just nodded. We were both a little drunk and I did not quite know what to make of her at that point. I talked to her for a while and found out enough about her to deduce she was intelligent and I was attracted to her. I had fallen for another blue-eyed girl. I just hoped this one was not riddled with "issues." Just then a tall redhead darted toward me. She grabbed me and said, "Your friend needs help!"

I thought to myself, "What friend? Jasmine is right here."

I had forgotten about Amber, whom I barely knew, upsetting her ex-girlfriend inside the bar.

I reluctantly said good-bye to Stefanie and went back inside to find nothing but a verbal fight in progress. I grabbed Amber who was yapping like a high-pitched Maltese on crack and forced her out of the bar where the party was. We went next door to a quieter venue and Amber quickly adapted to the new environment, buying Jaz a drink and trying to get into her top. As soon as they were safely settled down together I ran back to the other bar to find Stefanie. Before I could locate her I was grabbed by a big black woman on the way in who said, "You're mine, girl, it's my birthday and we're dancin'!" I was tousled back and forth between her and her two-hundred-pound friend until I could take no more. I said, "Happy birthday," gave her a quick hug and spotted my target. Stefanie was surprised to see me but when I told her I had come looking for her, she grabbed me and kissed me. Apparently she asked for my number, too, because she called me two days later.

Amber was an "I want my cake and to eat you too" kind of girl. She wanted Margarite around because she bought her a new BMW and paid the rent—in short she wanted the devotion that only an attentive partner can provide. But Amber also wanted to go out and have her fun and chase the impossible dream, the elusive bisexual Jasmine. Amber was dishonest and downright cruel to Margarite. The lesbian scene in LA is a very small and incestuous world; I found out later that Margarite was the ex of another lesbian friend of mine. I don't feel pity for

Katie Moran

Margarite for letting herself be abused by a girlfriend that blatantly cheats on her and relentlessly squeezes her for money; however, I do feel sorry for her because she, like so many women, is emotionally sick enough to take it. Margarite had cheated on my friend to be with Amber—all these women hated each other and did malicious things to one another and then would go out and get wasted together on Santa Monica Boulevard.

After a few outings with these freaks I slammed the door and locked it on any chance of friendship with them. With work, family, and real friends who has time to deal with psychotic acquaintances? Bobby sure had something to say about it. "Honey, listen to me. Dykes are just like fags with all the same drama but without the pretty faces, beautiful bodies and winning personalities." I think he was saying that just to get me to have lunch with him more often, which was fine. He was right, not about all lesbians but about this particular circle of women. There was no benefit in spending time with these people.

The horrors the evening produced were worth it for having met Stefanie. I had not been on a date with anyone for two years, since my first date with Carlo. I instinctively remembered what to do but I was still nervous the entire time. The first time we messed around I felt like such a loser. I was self-conscious about my body and what I was doing. It was like an out-of-body experience for me—I am usually the assertive one, with both men and women. I am like a tap dancer who knows where my foot will land every time, even when I am spinning in the air. Some would say that I've "got game." But my player days had been on hiatus for over for two years. When I dated Carlo, I closed the door on all of the escapades. I never thought I would be with another person again but here I was, face to face with a human being entirely different from Carlo.

And she was not shy. I asked her, "Are you nervous?" She laughed and said a definite, "No . . . are you?" I was and I admitted that to her. She could not understand why. I did not want to talk about my ex and not being with anyone in a while and all that other baggage I try to steer clear of. She was the girl that I once was, confident yet compassionate. I knew I could be that person once again and I transformed back that night. I even got up the balls to tell her that I was not ready for a relationship and I meant it.

I imagined that I might be sleeping with Jeannia, the girl with the huge tits from Newport Beach, or John, the gorgeous blonde who strolls around the office slowly, stopping by my desk long enough so that I can smell the Tancho in his hair and the cologne on his neck. He smells so great I want to lick his face. It would not be fair to Stefanie or myself to jump right back into a new relationship after being broken up for not quite a month. Stefanie was certainly someone I would consider dating seriously, she is an amazing person, but I had smelled freedom and it smelled like freshly washed hair or men's cologne. I was not turning back now.

I had not just opened the doors; I had opened the gates to heaven. I had a long way to go before I would be able to settle down. I knew I would find the right person, or maybe I already had. Maybe there is more than one. I knew there were certain avenues I would not be exploring **again**.

I had been hooked like a junkie to crack when it came to difficult yet beautiful women. So many of my relationships with both men and women have been fantastically catastrophic. I know a lot of women who have the struggle with those infamous bad boy types. Some women like bad boys; I like bad-for-me girls. They always seem to catch my eye. My photo albums looked like something out of Hef's family portrait. My ex-lover Seth always laughed at my struggle—he shared the same problems chasing women from coast to coast, thinking that they might be "the one."

The thing is, no matter how many times it has been said, the

Katie Moran

whole deal is really just about love. All the complications, the pain, the ups and downs are rooted in this very simple under-lying search for our human right—love. In the movie *Moulin Rouge*, the phrase "The greatest thing you'll ever learn is just to love and be loved in return" was repeated ad naseum, sure. But it is true nonetheless.

But for now I have a temp lying in bed next to me. He is a person just occupying the space until I am ready to meet the next love of my life. Maybe this person will not want me to rein in my parade of fun and festivities. The guy next to me knows that he is not there to stay, as he lies in bed looking out the window on a rainy New Orleans night. In the next moment he is up and dressed, and we go down to a bar on Bourbon Street to play a game of air hockey. Hey, in all the drama and confu-sion in the world sometimes a girl just needs to escape and have a little fun. Why close the door on that?

Off for Now

I could summarize all the stories I have talked about in some clever know-it-all phrase like "just be yourself, love who you are, and find your inner sexual voice." And, although that may be true, it is really all the messed-up things that I have done in and out of the bedroom that make me laugh today. All those times that I didn't go with my instincts and ended up getting totally screwed over seem to stick out the most. One thing I learned that has made me the person I am today is that you have to fall really hard to appreciate the good that life has to offer. I have chased many a loser only to have my heart completely broken. But then I was so much more appreciative when the right person came by and peeled my sorry ass off the pavement.

I love my friends, and the ones who have staying power in my life are the ones with good hearts—the honest ones. And I have watched all of them go through boyfriends, girlfriends, husbands, wives, threesomes, and foursomes. From the prom dress to the wedding dress and everything in between, I have watched my friends come into their own sexuality. I am still trying to get one friend of mine to let his fiancée stick her finger in his ass during intercourse but that's just me. I am persistent and I want people to never stop exploring their sexual tastes. There is nothing worse than a stagnant and sour sex life. My mother always says, "A good sex life adds to a relationship; it's a small but fulfilling part of it. But a bad sex life . . . a bad sex life takes up the entire relationship because it's impossible to forget its existence!" I think that is very true.

My mission has been to learn as much about myself and my partners as possible so that sex becomes just very natural, like breathing. The thing to remember is to just be aware. Make sex a lifelong curriculum. Learn what it is that turns you on and bring it to you. I am still finding out, as we are always changing as human beings. I have been in a relationship now for a few months and it is fabulous. I am taking it slow and not committing to just this one person; I am keeping my options open. And as for Carlo, there is a woman in his life that he finally listens to . . . his therapist. He hasn't had a drink in four months, so I am seeing him, too. It's like it was in the beginning—fun and pure-hearted. I still have a wandering eye for those hockey players. During sex sometimes I close my eyes and picture a puck flying into a net and a crowd cheering. Hey, do whatever works for you and do it safely. And for god's sake . . . replace the batteries in that damn vibrator!